MBE:

Beginning Your Campaign to Pass the Bar Exam

KEITH ELKIN

Dean of Students
Penn State Law

About Wolters Kluwer Law & Business

Wolters Kluwer Law & Business is a leading global provider of intelligent information and digital solutions for legal and business professionals in key specialty areas, and respected educational resources for professors and law students. Wolters Kluwer Law & Business connects legal and business professionals as well as those in the education market with timely, specialized authoritative content and information-enabled solutions to support success through productivity, accuracy and mobility.

Serving customers worldwide, Wolters Kluwer Law & Business products include those under the Aspen Publishers, CCH, Kluwer Law International, Loislaw, Best Case, ftwilliam.com and MediRegs family of products.

CCH products have been a trusted resource since 1913, and are highly regarded resources for legal, securities, antitrust and trade regulation, government contracting, banking, pension, payroll, employment and labor, and healthcare reimbursement and compliance professionals.

Aspen Publishers products provide essential information to attorneys, business professionals and law students. Written by preeminent authorities, the product line offers analytical and practical information in a range of specialty practice areas from securities law and intellectual property to mergers and acquisitions and pension/benefits. Aspen's trusted legal education resources provide professors and students with high-quality, up-to-date and effective resources for successful instruction and study in all areas of the law.

Kluwer Law International products provide the global business community with reliable international legal information in English. Legal practitioners, corporate counsel and business executives around the world rely on Kluwer Law journals, looseleafs, books, and electronic products for comprehensive information in many areas of international legal practice.

Loislaw is a comprehensive online legal research product providing legal content to law firm practitioners of various specializations. Loislaw provides attorneys with the ability to quickly and efficiently find the necessary legal information they need, when and where they need it, by facilitating access to primary law as well as state-specific law, records, forms and treatises.

Best Case Solutions is the leading bankruptcy software product to the bankruptcy industry. It provides software and workflow tools to flawlessly streamline petition preparation and the electronic filing process, while timely incorporating ever-changing court requirements.

ftwilliam.com offers employee benefits professionals the highest quality plan documents (retirement, welfare and non-qualified) and government forms (5500/PBGC, 1099 and IRS) software at highly competitive prices.

MediRegs products provide integrated health care compliance content and software solutions for professionals in healthcare, higher education and life sciences, including professionals in accounting, law and consulting.

Wolters Kluwer Law & Business, a division of Wolters Kluwer, is headquartered in New York. Wolters Kluwer is a market-leading global information services company focused on professionals.

This book is dedicated to my Mother,
who *always* believed in me,
and my late Father, the most intelligent and
generous man I will ever know.

About the Author

Keith Elkin is the Dean of Students at the Penn State University's Dickinson School of Law and teaches Fundamental Skills for the Bar Examination, a bar preparation course offered at Penn State Law. *Bar None* is based on his experience working with hundreds of bar exam candidates and the pedagogy of his course. Since he began teaching Fundamental Skills for the Bar Examination, the pass rate of students most at risk of failing the bar exam has doubled. Dean Elkin received a Bachelor's degree from Binghamton University, a Juris Doctor degree from the University of Miami, and a Master's degree in college administration, also from the University of Miami.

Contents

Preface and Acknowledgments

This book is designed to be used in bar preparation courses offered by law schools and for students who require more specialized instruction than commercial bar preparation courses provide in order to pass the bar exam. Candidates who previously failed a bar exam or are at risk[1] of failing based on poor law school performance will benefit from an early start and a supplemental approach to bar preparation. Foreign lawyers and others for whom English is a second language will also benefit from beginning their bar preparation well in advance of the bar exam.

Early bar preparation programs have the most benefit for students most at risk of failing. Most people pass the bar on their first attempt. Very good students will pass the bar exam whether or not they take an early preparation course because commercial bar preparation programs work well for most bar exam candidates. The typical commercial course begins approximately eight weeks before the bar exam and consists of watching videos of law professors providing instruction in the substantive law, studying subject matter outlines, and completing practice questions. This book is designed to be used in preparation for, not in lieu of, a commercial bar review course.

Preparing for the bar exam is hard work, requiring dedication and focused effort. Successful students typically study eight to ten hours a day during the eight weeks before the bar exam. There are no shortcuts or tricks to passing the bar. However, there are ways to become more efficient, effective, and strategic with the time you have to prepare. There are many commercial outlines widely available that cover the substantive law tested on the bar exam and provide practice questions and answers. It is not my intention to contribute to or replicate what already exists. My purpose

---

1. I am not using the term "at risk" in the pejorative. I use the term "at risk" to refer to students who for a variety of reasons are more likely to fail the bar exam than other students. At-risk students include, among others, those who have previously failed a bar exam, students ranking in the bottom quintile or so of their graduating class, those for whom English is not their first language, and students who have had to balance multiple responsibilities while in law school and may not have had the time to devote to their studies they otherwise would.

in writing this book is to explain how to think about organizing, learning, and applying the vast amount of material you must know in order to pass the bar exam.

When the American Bar Association began permitting law schools to offer bar exam preparation courses for credit, commercial providers were more than willing to sell course material to law schools and their students. Typically, these materials consist of a condensed version of their full eight-week commercial program. The benefit to the commercial providers is apparent. By using material that has already been prepared for another purpose, the cost of production is minimal. Moreover, providers use the opportunity to advertise their full course in an effort to solicit students who have not yet selected a commercial bar review course.

Starting bar preparation early is beneficial, *if it is the right type of preparation.* Offering a mini-commercial course is of little benefit to the vast majority of students who are going to pass the bar exam with or without an early start. There is a reason why bar preparation begins eight weeks before the exam: That timing works well for most students. Beginning the process two or four months earlier is of little substantive value to those students, although early exposure may serve to calm feelings of nervousness and the fear of the unknown. A mini-commercial course is also of little value to the at-risk students, who need more specialized instruction than the commercial courses provide. My approach is not to offer a course that is a mini-version of a commercial course but to prepare students for their commercial course by teaching them how to learn and study for the bar exam.

This book is based on my experience working with many at-risk students and on the pedagogy of the bar preparation course I teach at Penn State Law. My class is designed to teach students how to solve problems by focusing on at least one highly tested category in each MBE subject. I have taken the same approach in this book, which you will then be able to apply to other categories as you begin your full-time bar preparation.

I have found that the best way to learn the law and prepare for the MBE is through *wrong answers*, by learning from mistakes in the context of fact patterns rather than from substantive outlines. Since I began teaching bar preparation at Penn State, I have learned that an early start has virtually no impact on the pass rate for the overwhelming number of students. Most students will pass the bar on their first attempt with or without my course. But for those of you for whom law school was a struggle for whatever reason, my students who have been similarly situated pass the bar at a rate double than those who did not take my class prior to beginning their commercial course.

A significant reliance on outlines and videos in an early bar preparation course is easy for the teacher but is particularly ineffective for at-risk students. Regurgitation of the law is not the skill tested by the bar examiners.

While reading outlines and watching videos have a place in bar preparation, they are not as valuable for struggling students as designing an individualized strategy for approaching the exam, working through questions in an active and systematic manner, and learning a lot of substantive law through questions and answers, because the bar exam is fundamentally about problem solving.

This book begins by introducing students to the bar exam, offers approaches to organize the law for efficient study, and provides several important themes to keep in mind throughout bar exam preparation. Chapter 1 describes the bar exam itself and effective strategies and approaches to organizing your studies. Chapter 2 introduces the "broad lens" concept of reading bar exam questions, drawing from the organizational schemes described in Chapter 1, and provides application exercises. Chapter 3 focuses on the "narrow lens" concept: actively engaging with fact patterns by *asking*, not answering, questions. In Chapter 4, active preparation and learning is explained and demonstrated through answering a series of questions based on fact patterns. Chapter 5 highlights common mistakes students make by actively examining and learning from their errors. These are concepts in highly tested areas *you must understand* for bar exam success. This chapter is the capstone, bringing together the skills learned in the previous chapters. Finally, Chapter 6 provides some final tips as students begin their full-time preparation for the bar exam.

I wish to thank Penn State Law Dean Philip J. McConnaughay and Associate Dean Marie T. Reilly for the opportunity and privilege to teach and to my students who provided the inspiration for this book.

Keith Elkin
University Park, PA
March 2011

MBE:

Beginning Your Campaign to Pass the Bar Exam

Chapter 1

Introduction

A. The Bar Exam

Before beginning a substantive review of the law, examinees must have a thorough understanding of the structure of the bar exam. This is an integral part of being prepared, which encompasses more than substantive knowledge. You need to learn as much as you can about the exam before you can effectively design a strategy to pass.

So let's start with understanding the components of the bar exam. In most states, the bar examination is given twice a year, on the last Tuesday and Wednesday of February and July. The bar exam is actually comprised of two separate exams, the state exam and the Multistate Bar Exam (MBE). The state exam is typically comprised of essay questions, while the MBE is made up of multiple choice questions. The MBE is tested on Wednesday and the state exam is typically given the day before or the day after the MBE. Other states, like California, administer the test over three days.[1] Your score on the bar exam is made up of some combination of your state exam score and your MBE score, with their relative weight determined by each state.

Many states give the MBE and the state exam equal weight. However, there are exceptions. For example in Pennsylvania, the state exam counts for 55 percent of the total score, while the MBE makes up 45 percent of the score. In New York, the state exam is worth 60 percent of the total bar exam score. In California, the state exam counts for 65 percent of the total score.[2]

In addition to the state exam and the MBE, virtually every jurisdiction requires a passing score on the Multistate Professional Responsibility Exam (MPRE). The MPRE is made up of 60 multiple choice questions testing rules of professional conduct, with the passing threshold determined by each state. Most students take the MPRE while they are still in law school.[3]

---

1. See www.ncbex.org/bar-admissions/offices/ for a comprehensive listing of links to state bar admission offices. Each state provides detailed information about their specific requirements for bar admission, testing dates, locations, and the like.

2. See www.ncbex.org/fileadmin/mediafiles/downloads/Comp_Guide/CompGuide_2010.pdf for the weight each state assigns to the components of the bar exam.

3. Information about the MPRE can be found online at www.ncbex.org/multistate-tests/mpre/.

B. The MBE

The MBE is comprised of 200 multiple choice questions, of which 190 count in your score. The other 10 questions are experimental and do not count. You will not be able to pick out the experimental questions, so assume that all 200 questions count. These questions will cover six broad subject areas: constitutional law, contracts, criminal law and procedure, evidence, real property, and torts. There are 33 questions in torts and contracts, and 31 questions in each of the four remaining subjects. Your score is based on the number of questions you answer correctly. Each question is worth one point and there is no penalty for wrong answers; you should answer every question on the exam, even if you have to guess. The exam is broken into two 3-hour sessions, morning and afternoon, with a lunch break in between. Each session will have 100 questions.

The National Conference of Bar Examiners, the organization responsible for designing the MBE, further divides each subject into categories.[4] For example, torts is divided into intentional torts, negligence, strict liability, products liability, and other torts. Constitutional law is divided into individual rights, federalism, the separation of powers, and the nature of judicial review. You are responsible for a total of 30 categories, all of which will be tested, within the six subjects. However, the 30 categories are not treated equally. Some categories are more heavily tested than others. For example, you will see approximately four times as many negligence questions than questions on the admissibility of writings, recordings, and photos.

C. "Campaigning" to Pass the Bar Exam

Preparing for the bar exam is similar to running for president. To win election, a candidate does not need to win every state or even spend time in every state. In fact, it is bad strategy to spend an equal amount of time in every state because some states are worth more than others.[5] In order to

---

4. See www.ncebx.org/multistate-tests/mbe/ for an outline of the subject matter covered on the MBE. While each of the 30 categories will appear on the MBE, there is no guarantee which subcategories you will see.

5. In the United States, the president is not elected by a nationwide popular vote. The popular vote in each state determines which candidate "wins" that state. If each state was weighted equally, and assuming two candidates were running for election, a candidate would need to win the popular vote in 26 of the 50 states to be elected president. However, all states are not treated equally. The population of each state determines how much influence it has in the election process. The number of votes each state has ranges from 3 to 55. With a total number of votes available currently set at 538, a candidate would win election with 270 votes. As a result, a candidate doesn't need to win the popular vote in more than half of the states in order to win the election.

maximize their chances for election, presidential candidates typically focus on the states with the most electoral votes. Think of the 30 MBE categories as states, some of which are worth more than others. The strategic part of your "campaign" is to balance the relative worth of each of the 30 categories with your strengths and weaknesses in those areas.

Following are the 30 categories of law for which you will be responsible along with the approximate number of questions for each that you should expect on the bar exam.

1. Negligence (16-17)
2. Individual rights (15-16)
3. Constitutional protections afforded the accused (15-16)
4. Hearsay (10-11)
5. Presentation of evidence (10-11)
6. Formation of contracts (8-9)
7. Performance, breach, and discharge of contracts (8-9)
8. Property ownership (5-7)
9. Rights in land (5-7)
10. Real estate contracts (5-7)
11. Mortgages and security instruments (5-7)
12. Property titles (5-7)
13. The nature of judicial review (5-6)
14. Separation of powers (5-6)
15. Federalism (5-6)
16. Intentional torts (4-5)
17. Strict liability (4-5)
18. Products liability (4-5)
19. Other torts (4-5)
20. Defenses to contract enforceability (4-5)
21. Parol evidence (4-5)
22. Contract remedies (4-5)
23. Third-party contract rights (4-5)
24. Homicide (4-5)
25. Other crimes (4-5)
26. Inchoate crimes; parties (4-5)
27. General principles of criminal law (4-5)
28. Relevancy and reasons for excluding relevant evidence (3-4)
29. Privileges and other policy exclusions (3-4)
30. Admissibility of writings, recordings, and photos (3-4)

Notice that the *first seven categories* make up about 40 percent of the MBE questions. It is therefore quite evident that spending an equal amount of time and effort preparing for each of the 30 categories tested on the bar exam is an extremely poor strategy. *Moreover, it is a common mistake among unsuccessful test-takers.* Much like presidential candidates, who may choose not to spend any time campaigning in states with only a few electoral votes or states they know they cannot win, a bar exam candidate may strategically decide to "concede" certain categories or subcategories because the time and effort required to adequately prepare far exceeds their possible point value. Presidential candidates do not have to win every state to be elected president and bar exam candidates do not need to master the subject matter in all 30 categories to become licensed attorneys.

That said, there are certain categories bar exam candidates do not have the option of conceding, and part of a successful strategy of the bar exam is that recognition along with a willingness to put forth the utmost dedicated and focused effort in those areas, despite a possible lack of interest or strong capacity in the subject matter. In my experience, students at risk of failing the bar exam for any reason must do reasonably well (get more than 70 percent correct) in the categories making up 5 percent or more of the questions on the exam. In election terms, these are the "must wins":

1. Negligence (16-17)
2. Individual rights (15-16)
3. Constitutional protections afforded the accused (15-16)
4. Hearsay (10-11)
5. Presentation of evidence (10-11)
6. Formation of contracts (8-9)
7. Performance, breach, and discharge of contracts (8-9)

After these seven categories, examinees have some flexibility, if strategically exercised. With the remaining 23 categories, the goal is to maximize areas of strength and identify *a few* areas of weakness, which are reasonable to concede in the interest of using a finite period of preparation time efficiently and effectively.

Property is clustered among five categories (#8-12). If the thought of future interests gives you hives, concede it. Future interests are not even a category, but rather a subcategory of ownership. The rule against perpetuities (RAP) is a "sub-subcategory" of ownership. If you find this area particularly difficult, concede it. *You can pass the bar exam without mastering the RAP!* You may not even see a related question on the exam. Or, learn a few nuggets — like the rule doesn't apply to vested remainders — which may be helpful to eliminate one of the answer choices and increase your odds of selecting the right answer. **It is counterproductive to learn difficult, rarely or minimally tested areas of law for the following** *three* **reasons:**

1. The amount of time necessary to do well is highly disproportionate to the number of questions you are likely to see.

2. The opportunity cost is too high. Time spent on these areas is time you are not using to maximize the number of points you may achieve in much more highly tested areas.

3. Remaining positive and confident are important components of bar exam success. You must not become frustrated with a relatively inconsequential topic at the cost of losing confidence in your ability to do well in other, more important areas!

In summary, your campaign to pass the bar exam should consist of doing very well in the first seven MBE categories, maximizing areas of strength among the rest, and identifying a few areas you are willing to concede because of the high opportunity cost and strategic realization that it is not only not necessary, but also counterproductive, to try to learn everything that could possibly be tested in order to pass.

D. State Essay Exams

Your state exam counts for at least half of your total score on the bar exam. The bar examiner website for your jurisdiction will list the areas you are responsible for and in some cases provide questions and answers from past exams. There is a wealth of information on these sites, including the number of questions you should expect in the actual exam and the amount of time you should dedicate to studying for each category. It is well worth your time to learn as much as you can about your state exam before delving into the substantive law. I mentioned earlier that you could concede future interests on the MBE, but that may not be the case on your state essay exam. Like the MBE, learning about the state exam will help determine the best way to prepare. In other words, *prepare like a lawyer*, who learns as much as she can about the court, judge, and her adversary before trying a case.

If you plan to take the Pennsylvania Bar Exam, would it help your preparation if I told you that not only will property and contracts be tested, but they will be tested together in essay question five, where you will see exactly two main issues for each subject? Or that question one will test exactly these three categories: decedents' estates, federal income tax, and professional responsibility? Or that question two will have a criminal law component? How do I know? I went to the Pennsylvania website and read the past seven essay exams, which are publicly available.[6]

Part of the strategy of the bar exam is putting yourself in the best position to pass by knowing as much about the exam as possible in addition to the law. If you are taking the bar exam in Pennsylvania and spot only one

---

6. See www.pabarexam.org/bar_exam_information/essay.htm/.

major property issue in question five, your knowledge of the exam will compel you to go back over the question very carefully because you know it is extremely likely you missed something very important.

E. Organizing Material to Learn and Remember the Law

While it is bad strategy and counterproductive to try to learn every nuance about every subject tested on the bar exam, you need a way to organize and think about the vast amount of material you do need to remember. Again, there are no shortcuts to learning the substantive law. It takes time and dedicated focus. One way not to get overwhelmed by the amount of material is to think broadly about a subject and then narrow your focus; of course, the narrower the better because the bar exam tests details, not broad concepts. We already started organizing the material into categories. You should be able to organize each category in a manageable way to learn and review the substantive law. You will see later that this method of organization is particularly useful when actively reading and thinking about fact patterns.

It is beyond the purview of this book to cover or organize every category tested on the MBE. The goal here is to introduce some effective methods to organize, remember, and apply the law in a few highly tested categories. This foundation will allow you to build on, modify, or develop your own methods as you move into your commercial course. The two methods many students find most useful are 1) a modified outline approach that stimulates memory by asking a series of questions and 2) the use of charts and tables. Examples of each follow.

1. The Outline Approach

a. Negligence

Let's take the elements of a negligence claim. Every first-semester law student can recite the elements at the broadest level:

1. Duty
2. Breach
3. Causation
4. Damages

As you probably learned early in law school, this level of understanding doesn't get you very far. One needs to know more about each element and, even more importantly, how each applies when analyzing a fact pattern. By asking questions about each element, you'll move toward finer and more specific knowledge, which can then be applied on the bar exam. As you will see, asking questions while reading is critical to effective bar preparation.

1. Duty
   Is there a duty and to whom is it owed?
2. Breach
   What is the nature of the duty?
3. Causation
   Was there actual cause?
   Was there proximate cause?
   Is there a proof of fault problem?
4. Damages
   Did plaintiff suffer damages?

And further still:

1. Duty
   Is there a duty and to whom is it owed?
     Was the plaintiff foreseeable?
     Was there a duty to act?
     Was there a duty to control the conduct of someone else?
2. Breach
   What is the nature of the duty?
     Is there a statute?
     Is defendant in a special class?
3. Causation
   Was there actual cause?
     Was there one cause or multiple causes?
     Was there one tortfeasor or multiple tortfeasors?
   Was there proximate cause?
     Was the harm foreseeable?
     Was there a subsequent act of negligence that caused harm which was foreseeable?
   Is there a proof of fault problem?
     Does res ipsa loquitur apply?
     Did plaintiff meet the burden of production and establish a prima facie case?
4. Damages
   Did plaintiff suffer damages?
     What was the nature of the damages?
     Is there a limitation on liability?
     Are there multiple defendants?
     Does defendant have a defense?

Thinking of each category as a series of questions expends the breadth and depth of one's knowledge. One may get more and more detailed with this approach, but at the same time keep the material manageable. The goal is to use the broader concepts as "triggers" to remember the nuances. Organizing the material as a series of questions acts as an effective way to remember and apply the law on the bar exam. For example, the question "Is there a statute?" might trigger negligence per se, so you would know you need to determine whether the statute was designed to protect against the type of harm that occurred in the fact pattern and whether the plaintiff was a member of the class intended to be protected by the statute.

Over time, you will be able to considerably shorten your outline. Take the element of breach. Knowing that the standard of care may vary, one asks whether the defendant is in a special class. As you begin your bar preparation, you may be stuck here and need to take it further because knowing that the standard of care may vary with the defendant isn't enough without knowing what kinds of defendants are in a special class and what level of care applies. For example, you may need to further break down "special class" before triggering the level of care to apply.

> *Is the defendant in a special class?*
> *Is the defendant a professional?*
> *Is the defendant a child?*
> *Is the defendant a landowner?*
> *Is the defendant physically handicapped?*

The word "child" may then trigger the level of care: Children are held to the standard of care of a child of the same or similar age, intelligence, and experience unless engaged in adult activities.

b. Hearsay

Hearsay is another important category for which asking a series of questions works very well. Of course, the definition is critical: Hearsay is an out of court statement offered to prove the truth of the matter asserted and is inadmissible unless an exclusion or exception applies. The first two general questions should be fairly obvious: (1) Was there an out of court statement, and (2) if yes, was that statement offered for its truth value? Following is a fairly standard set of questions to begin a hearsay outline.

1. Was there an out of court *statement*? The emphasis on "statement" is to indicate that it is the trigger to remember to think broadly. Statements are not limited to oral or written words; for example, conduct such as a head nod may be considered a "statement."
2. Why was the statement offered? Statements may be offered for one of two reasons: (1) their truth value or (2) their value, regardless of truth. Asking *why* a statement was offered acts as a trigger to remember that if a statement is offered for a reason other than its truth, it is not hearsay. (It may still be inadmissible, but for another reason.)

3. If the statement was offered for its truth value, is that statement excluded by definition from the hearsay rule and therefore *not hearsay*?

4. If the statement was offered for its truth value, does the statement meet the requirements for an exception and therefore is admissible *despite being hearsay*?

5. If the statement qualifies under an exception as admissible hearsay, does that exception *require* the unavailability of the declarant at trial?

c. Contract Formation

The question approach also works well with the formation of contracts. Following is one approach; you'll need to determine how much or little detail works for you, and remember to be flexible.

i. Offer

1. Does the common law or Uniform Commercial Code (UCC) apply?
2. Was this an offer or an inquiry, advertisement, or solicitation for offers?
3. Was the offer irrevocable or temporarily irrevocable?
4. Did the offer specify a specific manner for acceptance?

ii. Acceptance

5. Was the offer accepted?
6. If this is a common law case, was the acceptance a mirror image of the offer?
7. If this is a UCC case, were there conflicting or additional terms?
8. Do the additional terms become part of the contract?
9. If the goods were nonconforming, was this an acceptance and breach or a counteroffer?
10. Did the power to accept terminate?
11. When did the acceptance become effective?

iii. Consideration

12. Were the terms of the contract definite?
13. Was there a bargained-for exchange of promises?
14. Are the promises enforceable without consideration?
15. Did the parties modify the terms of the contract?

2. Organizing with Charts and Tables

Another effective organizational approach is charting. The important point to keep in mind is that the method you use to organize and remember the law is a means to an end, not the end itself. These organizational methods are a tool that must be applied in the context of fact patterns. Many students who fail the bar exam make the mistake of spending far too much time on the means (memorizing their outlines) rather than the ends (doing practice questions). While it is necessary to learn the rules of football before you play, you will not increase your football skills by reading books. You get better by applying what you know on the field and by learning from your mistakes. The same concept applies here. Knowing the law is a necessary foundation, but the way to increase your score on the bar exam is by practicing the bar exam and learning from your mistakes.

I find charting especially useful to remember some of the distinctions between common law contracts and UCC Article 2:

a. Common Law Contracts versus UCC Article 2

Distinction	Common Law Contracts	UCC Article 2
Subject Matter	Services, intangibles, real estate	Goods
Open Items	Essential terms: parties, subject matter, price, quantity, time of performance	Gap fillers, if there is a reasonable basis for giving an appropriate remedy (Exception: must have a quantity term; output or requirement will satisfy)
Revocability	Revocable at will despite assurances to the contrary, unless supported by consideration	A firm offer (signed writing by a merchant + explicit assurance) may not be revoked for the stated period up to three months; consideration is not necessary
Additional Items	"Mirror image" rule; if acceptance deviates in any manner = rejection and counteroffer	Merchants: additional terms are presumptively part of the contract. If one or both not a Merchant: additional terms become part of the contract only if offeror assents
Conflicting Terms	Nonconforming acceptance is a rejection and counteroffer	"Knock-out" rule: conflicting terms are disregarded or knocked out; may use a gap filler
Modification	"Pre-existing duty" rule: modification solely benefiting one party is unenforceable due to lack of consideration; exception for unknown/ unforeseeable circumstances	Modifications made in good faith do not require consideration to be binding

b. Constitutional Rights

Many individual rights questions turn on knowing and applying the correct constitutional test or level of scrutiny a court will give to a statute. Rather than a series of questions, charting the right and the corresponding test is a very useful way to organize this category, particularly for visual learners.

Constitutional Area	Constitutional Test (Means/Ends)
Content-based speech	Strict scrutiny
Content-neutral speech	Intermediate scrutiny
Speech in a public forum	Narrowly drawn/significant interest + alternative avenues remain open
Speech in a nonpublic forum	Rational basis
Content-based commercial speech (truthful)	Quasi-intermediate scrutiny
Religion: Establishment Clause	Secular purpose + primary effect does not advance religion + no excessive government entanglement with religion
Religion: free exercise	Intentional interference = strict scrutiny Generally applicable law = rational basis
Fundamental rights ("privacy"): right to marry, procreate, live with family, and raise and educate your children	Strict scrutiny
Abortion	Previability: undue burden; postviability: exception to preserve woman's life and health
Right to vote	Strict scrutiny
Right to interstate travel	Strict scrutiny
Equal protection: suspect classifications (race, alienage, national origin)	Strict scrutiny
Equal protection: quasi-suspect classifications (gender, illegitimacy)	Intermediate scrutiny
Procedural due process	Balancing test between private and government interests
Government takings of private property	Public use + just compensation

In addition to your campaign plan for the MBE, you should develop an organizational approach that works best for you. That plan might differ from category to category, as seen by the approaches above. You need to find the best way to organize, learn, and remember legal principles so you can then apply the law to fact patterns. The outlines you make and receive from your commercial course provider are the tools in your active preparation for the bar exam. Remember, a common mistake made by unsuccessful bar exam candidates is spending far too much time organizing, learning, and remembering the law at the expense of "doing the bar exam" — systematically working through practice questions and answers. The bar examiners are not testing your ability to remember and repeat the material in outlines or commercial videos. Rather, the skill you must develop is applying the law to the types of fact patterns that make up the bar exam.

F. Important Points to Keep in Mind

1. **The *best time* to pass the bar exam is the *first time*.** The odds of passing a bar exam do not increase the second time around; in fact, the opposite is true. Across jurisdictions, one's odds of passing *decrease* dramatically with each attempt. Do not take the bar exam until you are ready. If you are preparing with the mind-set, "I can always take the test again if I fail" or "Hillary Clinton and John F. Kennedy, Jr. failed the bar, but eventually passed," you are preparing to fail.

2009 Pennsylvania Passing Rates for Specific Attempts[7]

	Successful	Unsuccessful	Pass Rate
1st Attempt	1,580	230	87.29%
2nd Attempt	21	40	34.43%
3rd Attempt	11	33	25.00%
4th Attempt +	11	71	13.41%

2. **Strategy is just as important as the substantive law on the bar exam.** You must focus your preparation on the most heavily tested topics first, maximize your areas of strength in others, and identify a few categories or subcategories that are reasonable to concede because of the disproportionate amount of time it would take to learn the material relative to the number of questions you are likely to see on the bar exam.

3. **You will maximize your chances for success by reading very carefully.** You can avoid missing crucial points by minimizing careless

---

7. See www.pabarexam.org/pdf/statistics/july/j2009.pdf.

errors. You will see many examples of this throughout the book, both with respect to reading questions and answer choices.

4. **Preparation for the bar exam is an active sport, not one for couch potatoes.** You learn how to play golf by playing golf, not by reading about it. You prepare for the bar exam by doing the bar exam, not by reading about it. Systematically going through questions and answer choices, and understanding why wrong answers are wrong, even if you answered the question correctly, will not only increase your substantive knowledge of the law but also your understanding of how it is applied, or misapplied, on actual questions. Likewise with your state essay questions. Many commercial companies encourage students to only outline their essay answers because it is easier for them to provide you feedback and you can get through more of them. However, outlining answers is not the skill on which you will be tested and you should write complete answers for every subject on your state exam, at least twice.

5. **"D=Esq."** You are not trying to get an A or a B on the bar exam. You can miss more than 30 percent of the questions on the bar exam and still pass. The bar exam is "pass/fail" and it doesn't matter if you pass by 1 point or 50 points, as long as you pass. No one will ever ask for your bar exam score, just whether you passed.

6. **You don't have to know the Rule Against Perpetuities to pass the bar exam.** This is of course shorthand for remembering that you don't have to know everything, but you should know as much as possible about what's important.

7. **You can prepare simultaneously for the MBE and state essay questions.** This point is critical. Preparing for the MBE and preparing for state essays are not mutually exclusive. By doing the exercises in this book, you will be practicing the concise writing necessary for doing well on the state portion of your exam.

8. **Truth in Advertising.** Preparing for the bar exam is not particularly fun, exciting, interesting, or intellectually stimulating. But it is a requirement for entry into your chosen profession.

9. **Answering bar exam questions is a skill, and like most skills, you will only get better with practice.** The purpose of this book is to get you started.

Chapter 2

The Broad Lens:
Setting the Framework
for Legal Analysis

Knowledge and recall of the law is the first prerequisite to analysis and application, the fundamental skills tested by the bar exam. However, application of the law necessarily requires knowing what law to apply. Drawing from the organizational schemes described in Chapter 1, the broad lens provides the framework for the careful reading required for the deeper level of analysis necessary to answer questions, the subject of subsequent chapters.

The broad lens is similar to a law school case brief. A good brief is a tool to organize one's thinking about a case and provides the framework for analyzing hypothetical questions. For the bar exam, your broad lens will allow you to identify issues and rules in order to analyze fact patterns.

The broad lens has two components.

1. **Identifying the fundamental legal issue(s).** Questions on the bar exam are not labeled or organized by subject matter. The first step is to quickly categorize the substance of the fact pattern and hone in on the nature of the problem or the issue between the parties. For example, the fact pattern may be about negligence and the issue may be the duty of care of a child.
2. **Identifying the applicable legal rule.** Identification of the issue should trigger a general rule. If the issue is the duty of care of a child, the general rule is that children are held to the standard of a reasonably prudent child of the same age, intelligence, and experience unless engaged in adult activities.

You are responsible for remembering a lot of rules for the bar exam, some of which you will be re-learning and others that you will be learning for the first time. You will not know all of the rules that apply to the fact pattern exercises that follow but you should be able to state the legal issues in most of them. Consult a hornbook or other reference material for the substantive law as you complete the questions. You will find that it is much easier and more effective to remember rules *in the context of a fact pattern*, than by memorizing an outline without any context. This is an example of active preparation for the bar exam. You will be adding to your substantive knowledge by completing these exercises and will simultaneously be preparing for your state essay exam by practicing clear and concise writing.

In the exercise below, a question follows each fact pattern but there are no answer choices. The questions are useful to frame the legal issues but the answers are not necessary. The focus in this chapter is on constructing a framework for thinking about fact patterns, not on applying the rule to the facts and right and wrong answers. That will be the focus of subsequent chapters.

A. Sample Broad Lens Analysis I

A state statute requires any person licensed to sell prescription drugs to file with the State Board of Health a report listing the types and amounts of such drugs sold if his sales of such drugs exceed $50,000 during the calendar year. The statute makes it a misdemeanor to "knowingly fail to file" such a report. Nelson, who is licensed to sell prescription drugs, sold $63,000 worth of prescription drugs during 1976 but did not file the report. Charged with committing the misdemeanor, Nelson testified that he did a very poor job of keeping records and did not realize that his sales of prescription drugs had exceeded $50,000. If the jury believes Nelson he should be found

> *Comment:* Whenever I see a statute, I assume the question will turn on whether or not the statute was violated. I look for facts that would indicate a violation. Here, we are told that Nelson did a poor job of keeping records and didn't realize sales exceeded $50,000. Given these facts, I see that my assumption was correct because the issue will be whether Nelson formed the requisite intent in the statute ("knowingly") to commit the crime.

> **Concisely state the fundamental legal issue(s).**
> The issue is whether Nelson had the requisite intent, "knowingly," to be found guilty of the crime.

> **Concisely state the generally applicable legal rule.**
> A person acts knowingly when she is practically certain of the existence of the fact in question.

B. Sample Broad Lens Analysis II

Passer was driving his pickup truck along a lonely road on a very cold night. Passer saw Tom, who was a stranger, lying in a field by the side of the road and apparently injured. Passer stopped his truck, alighted, and, upon examining Tom, discovered that Tom was intoxicated and in danger of suffering from exposure to the cold. However, Passer returned to his truck and drove away without making any effort to help Tom. Tom remained lying at the same place and was later injured when a car driven by Traveler, who was drowsy and inattentive, veered off the road into the field and hit Tom. Traveler did not see Tom prior to hitting him. If Tom asserts a claim against Passer for damages for his injuries, will Tom prevail?

> *Comment:* On my first read through I could see this was a negligence question because there is a claim for damages for injuries. The fact that Passer did nothing raises the first element of any negligence claim: whether or not defendant owes plaintiff a duty of care. Whenever you are asked whether a plaintiff will prevail on a negligence claim, run through the elements of the prima facie case (duty, breach, causation, and damages). If plaintiff is unable to prove all four elements he loses.

Concisely state the fundamental legal issue(s).
The issue is whether Passer owes Tom a duty of care.

Concisely state the generally applicable legal rule.
The general rule is that, absent a special relationship, there is no duty to come to the rescue of someone in peril.

C. Broad Lens Exercises

1. A plaintiff sued a defendant under an age discrimination statute, alleging that the defendant refused to hire the plaintiff because she was over age 65. The defendant's defense was that he refused to employ the plaintiff because he reasonably believed that she would be unable to perform the job. The defendant seeks to testify that the plaintiff's former employer advised him not to hire the plaintiff because she was unable to perform productively for more than four hours a day. Is the testimony of the defendant admissible?

> *Hint:* Defendant is seeking to repeat a statement in court that was made to him out of court.

Concisely state the fundamental legal issue(s).

_____

_____

Concisely state the generally applicable legal rule.

_____

_____

_____

_____

2. Six years ago, Oscar, owner of Blackacre in fee simple, executed and delivered to Albert an instrument in the proper form of a warranty deed, purporting to convey Blackacre to "Albert and his heirs." At that time, Albert was a widower who had one child, Donna. Three years ago, Albert executed and delivered to Bea an instrument in the proper form of a warranty deed, purporting to convey Blackacre to "Bea." Donna did not join in the deed. Bea was and still is unmarried and childless. The only possibly applicable statute in the jurisdiction states that any deed will be construed to convey the grantor's entire estate, unless expressly limited. Last month, Albert died, never having remarried. Donna is his only heir. Blackacre is now owned by

> _Hint:_ Do Albert's heirs have a property interest?

Concisely state the fundamental legal issue(s).

_____

_____

Concisely state the generally applicable legal rule.

_____

_____

_____

_____

3. The governor of the state of Green proposes to place a Christmas nativity scene, the components of which would be permanently donated to
the state by private citizens, in the Green Capitol Building rotunda
where the Green Legislature meets annually. The governor further
proposes to display this state-owned nativity scene annually from
December 1 to December 31, next to permanent displays that depict
the various products manufactured in Green. The governor's proposal
is supported by all members of both houses of the legislature. If challenged in a lawsuit on Establishment Clause grounds, the proposed
nativity scene display would be held

Concisely state the fundamental legal issue(s).

_____

_____

Concisely state the generally applicable legal rule.

_____

_____

_____

_____

4. Albert engaged Bertha, an inexperienced actress, to do a small role in a
new Broadway play for a period of six months at a salary of $200 a week.
Bertha turned down another role in order to accept this engagement.
On the third day of the run, the Bertha was hospitalized with influenza
and Helen was hired to do the part. A week later Bertha recovered, but
Albert refused to accept her services for the remainder of the contract
period. Will Bertha be successful in an action brought against Albert for
breach of contract?

Concisely state the fundamental legal issue(s).

_____

_____

Concisely state the generally applicable legal rule.

_____

_____

_____

_____

5. In a federal investigation of Defendant for tax fraud, the grand jury seeks to obtain a letter written January 15 by Defendant to her attorney in which she stated: "Please prepare a deed giving my ranch to the local university but, in order to get around the tax law, I want it backdated to December 15." The attorney refused to produce the letter on the ground of privilege. Should production of the letter be prohibited?

Concisely state the fundamental legal issue(s).

_____

_____

Concisely state the generally applicable legal rule.

_____

_____

_____

_____

6. Morgan conveyed Greenacre to "Perez for life, remainder to Rowan, her heirs, and assigns, subject, however, to the mortgage thereon." The mortgage had an unpaid balance of $10,000, which is payable in $1,000 annual installments plus interest at 6 percent on the unpaid balance, with the next payment due on July 1. Perez is now occupying Greenacre. The reasonable rental value of the property exceeds the sum necessary to meet all current charges. There is no applicable statute. Under the rules governing contributions between life tenants and remaindermen, how should the burden for payment be allocated?

Concisely state the fundamental legal issue(s).

_____

_____

Concisely state the generally applicable legal rule.

_____

_____

_____

_____

7. While browsing in a clothing store, Alice decided to take a purse without paying for it. She placed the purse under her coat and took a couple of steps toward the exit. She then realized that a sensor tag on the purse would set off an alarm. She placed the purse near the counter from which she removed it. Has Alice committed a crime?

Concisely state the fundamental legal issue(s).

_____

_____

Concisely state the generally applicable legal rule.

_____

_____

_____

_____

8. The executive director of an equal housing opportunity organization was the leader of a sit-in at the offices of a real estate management company. The protest was designed to call attention to the company's racially discriminatory rental practices. When police demanded that the director desist from trespassing on the company's property, she refused and was arrested. In her trial for trespass, the prosecution peremptorily excused all non-whites from the jury, arguing to the court that even though the director was white, minority groups would automatically support her because of her fight against racism in housing accommodations. If the director is convicted of trespass by an all-white jury and appeals, claiming a violation of her constitutional rights, the court should?

Concisely state the fundamental legal issue(s).

_____

_____

Concisely state the generally applicable legal rule.

_____

_____

_____

_____

9. In a single writing, Painter contracted with Farmer to paint three identical barns on her rural estate for $2,000 each. The contract provided for

Farmer's payment of $6,000 upon Painter's completion of the work on all three barns. Painter did not ask for any payment when the first barn was completely painted, but she demanded $4,000 after painting the second barn. Assume that Farmer rightfully refused Painter's demand for payment. If Painter immediately terminates the contract without painting the third barn, what is Painter entitled to recover from Farmer?

Concisely state the fundamental legal issue(s).

_____

_____

Concisely state the generally applicable legal rule.

_____

_____

_____

_____

10. Si was in the act of siphoning gasoline from Neighbor's car in Neighbor's garage and without his consent when the gasoline exploded and a fire followed. Rescuer, seeing the fire, grabbed a fire extinguisher from his car and put out the fire, saving Si's life and Neighbor's car and garage. In doing so, Rescuer was badly burned. If Rescuer asserts a claim against Si for personal injuries, Rescuer will

Concisely state the fundamental legal issue(s).

_____

_____

Concisely state the generally applicable legal rule.

_____

_____

_____

_____

D. Broad Lens Exercise Answers

1. **Issue:** The issue is whether Employer's statement is hearsay.
   Rule: Hearsay is an out of court statement offered to prove the truth of the matter asserted therein, that Plaintiff was unable to work for more than four hours a day. Out of court statements offered for their truth value are inadmissible unless excluded by definition or an exception applies.

2. **Issue:** The issue is whether the conveyance from Albert to Bea was valid without Donna's participation in the transfer.
   Rule: A conveyance to a person and his heirs creates a fee simple absolute. No future interest is created and the holder of a fee simple absolute may sell, transfer, or otherwise dispose of that property without the permission or knowledge of his heirs.

3. **Issue:** The issue is whether the proposed display passes constitutional muster under the _Lemon_ test.
   Rule: Under the _Lemon_ test, state action will not violate the Establishment Clause if: (1) it has a secular purpose, (2) the action neither advances nor inhibits religion, and (3) the action does not cause excessive government entanglement with religion. Under current Supreme Court precedent, state-sponsored nativity scenes standing alone violate the _Lemon_ test. However, nativity scenes are not per se unconstitutional. If a nativity scene is part of a larger holiday display containing mainly secular symbols, like reindeer, snowmen, and the like, the display as a whole may not violate the Establishment Clause.

4. **Issue:** The issue is whether Bertha's breach was a material or minor breach.
   Rule: A court will consider a variety of factors in determining the nature of a breach such as, the length of partial performance, whether the breach was willful, and whether the party in breach was willing to complete the contract.

5. **Issue:** The issue is whether the attorney-client privilege applies to the communication here.

    Rule: The general rule is that confidential communications between lawyer and client in the course of their professional relationship are privileged and prevented from disclosure. However, there is an exception to the rule for services to aid in the commission of a crime.

6. **Issue:** The issue is how payment of the mortgage and the interest thereon is split between a life tenant and the holder of the future interest.

    Rule: The general rule is that the holder of a life estate pays the interest and the holder of the remainder pays the principal.

7. **Issue:** The issue is whether a change of mind negates the intent element of larceny.

    Rule: Larceny is the taking and carrying away the property of another with the intent to permanently deprive the other of that property. If the intent coincides with the act, the crime has been committed. A subsequent change of mind does not undo the crime.

8. **Issue:** The issue is whether the dismissal of all non-whites from the jury by the prosecutor violates the Equal Protection Clause of the Fourteenth Amendment.

    Rule: The rule is that jurors may not be dismissed if the exclusion is based only on race.

9. **Issue:** The issue is whether the party who breaches a contract is entitled to payment for part performance.

    Rule: If the breaching party has not rendered substantial performance, he may not recover at law but may recover in equity under *quantum meruit* ("as much as he deserves").

10. **Issue:** The issue is whether the rescuer assumed the risk of injury by voluntarily acting to put out the fire.

    Rule: The affirmative defense of assumption of risk does not apply to rescuers.

Chapter 3

The Narrow Lens: Actively Reading Fact Patterns

Actively engaging with fact patterns and thinking about legal principles as you read are critical components for success on the bar exam. Active engagement is using the "narrow lens" in conjunction with the framework provided by the broad lens and is focused to answer the question, **"Why is this important?"** as you read. Formulating questions while reading stimulates critical thinking and reasoning. Highlighting and underlining passages are passive approaches to analyzing bar exam questions and is a very poor strategy. Very good exam takers write notes to themselves in the margins of questions for later reference. At-risk students have a tendency to highlight and underline passages without really reading the material. Formulating questions forces examinees to process the information they are reading, a precursor to the solid legal analysis required for success on the bar exam.

As a general rule, you should assume that every bit of information in a fact pattern is relevant, and the narrow lens helps you think about why. Following are two examples that demonstrate the best way to actively engage with fact patterns.

A. Sample Narrow Lens Analysis I

Oxnard owned Goldacre, a tract of land, in fee simple. At a time when Goldacre was in the adverse possession of Amos, Eric obtained the oral permission of Oxnard to use as a road or driveway a portion of Goldacre to reach adjoining land, Twin Pines, which Eric owned in fee simple. Thereafter, during all times relevant to this problem, Eric used this road between Goldacre regularly for ingress and egress between Twin Pines and a public highway. Amos quit possession of Goldacre before acquiring title by adverse possession. Without any further communication between Oxnard and Eric, Eric continued to use the road for a total period — from the time he first began to use it — sufficient to acquire an easement by prescription. Oxnard then blocked the road and refused to permit its continued use. Eric brought suit to determine his right to continue use of the road. Eric should

> *Comment:* "Eric obtained the oral permission of Oxnard to use as a road or driveway a portion of Goldacre to reach adjoining land" raised two immediate questions for me: (1) Can oral permission create a valid property interest? The bar examiners could have told me simply that Eric had Oxnard's permission but they made a point of telling me the permission was oral. Why? (2) What type of interest did Oxnard convey? When I see a conveyance in any property question, I immediately ask myself what type of property interest was created and whether or not there is an accompanying future interest. We are also told that the Oxnard to Eric conveyance occurred while Amos was in adverse possession of Goldacre. This leads me to wonder if the adverse possession issue has any impact on the validity of the conveyance. Lastly, Amos quit possession before obtaining title, which leads me to the question of what effect, if any, this has on the relative property rights of Oxnard and Eric.

B. Sample Narrow Lens Analysis II

Albert engaged Bertha, an inexperienced actress to do a small role in a new Broadway play for a period of six months at a salary of $200 a week. Bertha turned down another role in order to accept this engagement. On the third day of the run, Bertha was hospitalized with influenza and Helen was hired to do the part. A week later, Bertha recovered, but Albert refused to accept her services for the remainder of the contract period. Bertha then brought an action against Albert for breach of contract. Which of the following is Bertha's best legal theory?

> *Comment:* Note that Bertha is not just an actress; she is an inexperienced actress. Why did the bar examiners make a point of telling me she was inexperienced? This leads me to question why her inexperience is relevant. Further, why are we told that Bertha turned down another opportunity? When I first read this question, I made a note here asking if turning down another role is an issue for damages. Lastly, I know this contract is governed by the common law because it does not involve the sale of goods. Under the common law, the question you need to ask is whether or not the breach was material.

C. Narrow Lens Exercises

With your broad lens providing the framework, write at least three questions you asked yourself as you actively read each of the following fact patterns.

1. Driving down a dark road, Defendant accidentally ran over a man. Defendant stopped and found that the victim was dead. Defendant, fearing that he might be held responsible, took the victim's wallet, which contained a substantial amount of money. He removed the identification papers and put the wallet and money back into the victim's pocket. Defendant is **not guilty** of

> *Hint:* Adverbs (and adjectives) almost always raise questions. Defendant didn't just run someone over, he accidentally *ran someone over.*

Question #1:_____

_____

Question #2:_____

_____

Question #3:_____

_____

2. Mom rushed her 8-year-old daughter, Child, to the emergency room at Hospital after Child fell off her bicycle and hit her head on a sharp rock. The wound caused by the fall was extensive and bloody. Mom was permitted to remain in the treatment room, and held Child's hand while the emergency room physician cleaned and sutured the wound. During the procedure, Mom said that she was feeling faint and stood up to leave the room. While leaving the room, Mom fainted and, in falling, struck her head on a metal fixture that protruded from the emergency room wall. She sustained a serious injury as a consequence. If Mom sues Hospital to recover damages for her injury, will she prevail?

> *Hint:* If someone is injured at a place of business or other establishment generally held open to the public, think about what duty is owed to the injured party.

Question #1:_____

_____

Question #2:_____

_____

Question #3:_____

_____

3. Reggie offered Harriet $200 for a 30-day option to buy Harriet's land, Grandvale, for $10,000. As Harriet knew, Reggie, if granted the option, intended to resell Grandvale at a profit. Harriet declined, believing that she could find a desirable purchaser herself. Reggie thereupon said to Harriet, "Make me a written, 30-day offer, revocable at your pleasure, to sell me Grandvale at a sale price of $10,000, and tomorrow I will pay you $200 for so doing." Harriet agreed and gave Reggie the following document: "For 30 days I offer my land known as Grandvale to Reggie for $10,000, this offer to be revocable at my pleasure at any time before acceptance. [Signed] Harriet." Later that day Harriet's neighbor, Norma, said to Harriet, "I know someone who would probably buy Grandvale for $15,000." Harriet asked, "Who?" and Norma replied, "My cousin Portia." Harriet thanked Norma. Several hours later, Norma telephoned Harriet and said, "Of course, if you sell to Portia I will expect the usual 5 percent brokerage fee for finding a buyer." Harriet made no reply. The next day Harriet telephoned Reggie, declared that her written offer to him was revoked, and demanded payment of $200. Reggie refused to pay. Harriet subsequently sold Grandvale to Portia for $15,000 but refused to pay Norma anything.

Question #1:_____

_____

Question #2:_____

_____

Question #3:_____

_____

4. Fernwood Realty Company developed a residential development, known as the Fernwood Development, which included single-family dwellings, town houses, and high-rise apartments for a total of 25,000 dwelling units. Included in the deed to each unit was a covenant under which the grantee and the grantee's "heirs and assigns" agreed to purchase electrical power only from a plant Fernwood promised to build and maintain within the development. Fernwood constructed the plant and the necessary power lines. The plant did not supply power outside the development. An appropriate and fair formula was used to determine price. After constructing and selling 12,500 of the units, Fernwood sold its interest in the development to Gaint Realty Investors. Gaint operated the power plant and constructed and sold the remaining 12,500 units. Each conveyance from Gaint contained the same covenant relating to electrical power that Fernwood had included in the 12,500 conveyances it had made. Page bought a dwelling unit from Olm, who had purchased it from Fernwood. Subsequently, Page, whose lot was along the boundary of the Fernwood development, ceased buying electrical power from Gaint and began purchasing power from General Power Company, which provided such service in the area surrounding the Fernwood development. Both General Power and Gaint have governmental authorization to provide electrical services to the area. Gaint instituted an appropriate action against Page to enjoin her from obtaining electrical power from General Power. Assume that the jurisdiction follows the traditional rule for the running of covenants. If judgment is for Page, it most likely will be because

Question #1:_____

_____

Question #2:_____

_____

Question #3:_____

_____

5. A generally applicable state statute requires an autopsy by the county coroner in all cases of death that are not obviously of natural causes. The purpose of this law is to ensure the discovery and prosecution of all illegal activity resulting in death. In the 50 years since its enactment, the statute has been consistently enforced. Mr. and Mrs. Long are sincere,

practicing members of a religion that maintains it is essential for a deceased person's body to be buried promptly and without any invasive procedures, including an autopsy. When the Longs' son died of mysterious causes and an autopsy was scheduled, the Longs filed an action in state court challenging the constitutionality of the state statute, and seeking an injunction prohibiting the county coroner from performing an autopsy on their son's body. In this action, the Longs claimed only that the application of this statute in the circumstances of their son's death would violate their right to the free exercise of religion as guaranteed by the First and Fourteenth Amendments. Assume that no federal statutes are applicable. As applied to the Longs' case, the court should rule that the state's autopsy statute

Question #1:_____

_____

Question #2:_____

_____

Question #3:_____

_____

6. At Dove's trial for theft, Mr. Wong, called by the prosecutor, testified to the following: (1) that from his apartment window, he saw thieves across the street break the window of a jewelry store, take jewelry, and leave in a car; (2) that Mrs. Wong telephoned the police and relayed to them the license number of the thieves' car as Mr. Wong looked out the window with binoculars and read it to her; (3) that he has no present memory of the number, but that immediately afterward he listened to a playback of the police tape recording giving the license number (which belongs to Dove's car) and verified that she had relayed the number accurately. Playing the tape recording for the jury would be

Question #1:_____

_____

Question #2:_____

_____

Question #3:_____

_____

7. At Defendant's trial for sale of drugs, the government called Witness to testify, but Witness refused to answer any questions about Defendant and was held in contempt of court. The government then calls Officer to testify that, when Witness was arrested for possession of drugs and offered leniency if he would identify his source, Witness had named Defendant as his source. The testimony offered concerning Witness's identification of Defendant is

Question #1:_____

_____

Question #2:_____

_____

Question #3:_____

_____

8. Martha's high school teacher told her that she was going to receive a failing grade in history, which would prevent her from graduating. Furious, she reported to the principal that the teacher had fondled her, and the teacher was fired. A year later, still unable to get work because of the scandal, the teacher committed suicide. Martha, remorseful, confessed that her accusation had been false. If Martha is charged with manslaughter, her best defense would be that she

Question #1:_____

_____

Question #2:_____   _____

_____

Question #3:_____

_____

9. Plaintiff's estate sued Defendant Stores claiming that Guard, one of
Defendant's security personnel, wrongfully shot and killed Plaintiff
when Plaintiff fled after being accused of shoplifting. Guard was convicted of manslaughter for killing Plaintiff. At his criminal trial, Guard,
who was no longer working for Defendant, testified that Defendant's
security director had instructed him to stop shoplifters "at all costs."
Because Guard's criminal conviction is on appeal, he refuses to testify at
the civil trial. Plaintiff's estate then offers an authenticated transcript of
Guard's criminal trial testimony concerning the instructions of Defendant's security director. This evidence is

Question #1:_____

_____

Question #2:_____

_____

Question #3:_____

_____

10. The following facts concern a tract of land in a state that follows general
U.S. law. Each instrument is in proper form, recorded, marital property
rights were waived when necessary, and each person named was adult
and competent at the time of the named transaction. In 1940, Oleg, the
owner, conveyed his interest in fee simple "to my brothers Bob and Bill,
their heirs and assigns as joint tenants with right of survivorship."
In 1950, Bob died, devising his interest to his only child, "Charles,
for life, and then to Charles's son, Sam, for life, and then to Sam's
children, their heirs and assigns." In 1970, Bill died, devising his interest
"to my friend, Frank, his heirs and assigns." In 1972, Frank conveyed his
quitclaim deed "to Paul, his heirs and assigns whatever right, title and
interest I own." Paul has never married. Paul has contracted to convey
marketable record title in the land to Patrick. Can Paul do so?

Question #1:_____

_____

Question #2:_____

_____

Question #3:_____

_____

11. Patron ate a spicy dinner at Restaurant on Sunday night. He enjoyed the food and noticed nothing unusual about the dinner. Later that evening, Patron had an upset stomach. He slept well through the night, went to work the next day, and ate three meals. His stomach discomfort persisted, and by Tuesday morning he was too ill to go to work. Eventually, Patron consulted his doctor, who found that Patron was infected with a bacterium that can be contracted from contaminated food. Food can be contaminated when those who prepare it do not adequately wash their hands. Patron sued Restaurant for damages. He introduced testimony from a health department official that various health code violations had been found at Restaurant both before and after Patron's dinner, but that none of Restaurant's employees had signs of bacterial infection when they were tested one month after the incident. Restaurant's best argument in response to Patron's suit would be that

> Hint: There's an adjective in the first sentence.

Question #1:_____

_____

Question #2:_____

_____

Question #3:_____

_____

12. A city owns and operates a large, public auditorium. It leases the auditorium to any group that wishes to use it for a meeting, lecture, concert, or contest. Each user must post a damage deposit and pay rent, which is calculated only for the actual time the building is used by the lessee. Reservations are made on a first-come, first-served basis. A private organization that permits only males to serve in its highest offices rented the auditorium for its national convention. The organization planned to install its new officers at that convention. It broadly publicized the event, inviting members of the general public to attend the installation ceremony at the city auditorium. No statute or administrative rule prohibits the organization from restricting its highest offices to men. An appropriate plaintiff sues the private organization seeking to enjoin it from using the city auditorium for the installation of its new officers. The sole claim of the plaintiff is that the use of this auditorium by the organization for the installation ceremony is unconstitutional because the organization disqualifies women from serving in its highest offices. Will the plaintiff prevail?

Question #1:_____

_____

Question #2:_____

_____

Question #3:_____

_____

13. At a party, Diane and Victor agreed to play a game they called "spin the barrel." Victor took an unloaded revolver, placed one bullet in the barrel, and spun the barrel. Victor then pointed the gun at Diane's head and pulled the trigger once. The gun did not fire. Diane then took the gun, pointed it at Victor, spun the barrel, and pulled the trigger once. The gun fired, and Victor fell over dead. A statute in the jurisdiction defines murder in the first degree as an intentional and premeditated killing or one occurring during the commission of a common law felony, and defines murder in the second degree as all other murder at common law. Manslaughter is defined as a killing in the heat of passion upon an adequate legal provocation or a killing caused by gross negligence. The most serious crime for which Diane can properly be convicted is

Question #1:_____

_____

Question #2:_____

_____

Question #3:_____

_____

14. On November 1, the following notice was posted in a privately operated law school: "The faculty, seeking to encourage legal research, offers to any student at this school who wins the current National Obscenity Law Competition the additional prize of $500. All competing papers must be submitted to the Dean's office before May 1. (The National Competition is conducted by an outside agency, unconnected with any law school.)" Student read this notice on November 2, and thereupon intensified his effort to make his paper on obscenity law, which he started in October, a winner. Student also left on a counter in the Dean's office a signed note saying, "I accept the faculty's $500 Obscenity Competition offer." This note was inadvertently placed in Student's file and never reached the Dean or any faculty member personally. On the following April 1, the above notice was removed and the following substituted therefore: "The faculty regrets that our offer regarding the National Obscenity Law Competition must be withdrawn." Student's paper was submitted through the Dean's office on April 15. On May 1, it was announced that Student had won the National Obscenity Law Competition and the prize of $1,000. The law faculty refused to pay anything. As to Student, was the offer effectively revoked?

Question #1:_____

_____

Question #2:_____

_____

Question #3:_____

_____

15. By the terms of a written contract signed by both parties on January 15, M.B. Ram, Inc., agreed to sell a specific ICB personal computer to Marilyn Materboard for $3,000, and Materboard agreed to pick up and pay for the computer at Ram's store on February 1. Materboard unjustifiably repudiated on February 1. Without notifying Materboard, Ram subsequently sold at private sale the same specific computer to Byte, who paid the same price ($3,000) in cash. The ICB is a popular product. Ram can buy from the manufacturer more units than it can sell at retail. If Ram sues Materboard for breach of contract, Ram will probably recover

Question #1:_____

_____

Question #2:_____

_____

Question #3:_____

_____

16. John is a licensed barber in State A. The State A barber licensing statute provides that the Barber Licensing Board may revoke a barber license if it finds that a licensee has used his or her business premises for an illegal purpose. John was arrested by federal narcotics enforcement agents on a charge of selling cocaine in his barbershop in violation of federal laws. However, the local U.S. Attorney declined to prosecute and the charges were dropped. Nevertheless, the Barber Licensing Board commenced a proceeding against John to revoke his license on the ground that John used his business premises for illegal sales of cocaine. At a subsequent hearing before the board, the only evidence against John was affidavits by unnamed informants, who were not present or available for cross-examination. Their affidavits stated that they purchased cocaine from John in his barbershop. Based solely on this evidence, the board found that John used his business premises for an illegal purpose and ordered his license revoked. In a suit by John to have this revocation set aside, his best constitutional argument is that

Question #1:_____

_____

Question #2:_____

_____

Question #3:_____

_____

17. Ben was the illegitimate, unacknowledged child of Fred. Fred died intestate, leaving neither spouse nor any children other than Ben. The state's law of intestate succession provides that an unacknowledged illegitimate child may not inherit his father's property. The spouse, all other blood relations, and the state are preferred as heirs over the unacknowledged illegitimate child. Ben filed suit in an appropriate court alleging that the state statute barring an illegitimate child from sharing in a parent's estate is invalid, and that he should be declared lawful heir to his father's estate. In challenging the validity of the state statute, Ben's strongest argument would be that

Question #1:_____

_____

Question #2:_____

_____

Question #3:_____

_____

18. Bill and Chuck hated Vic and agreed to start a fight with Vic and, if the opportunity arose, to kill him. Bill and Chuck met Vic in the street outside a bar and began to push him around. Ray, Sam, and Tom, who also hated Vic, stopped to watch. Ray threw Bill a knife. Sam told Bill, "Kill him." Tom, who made no move and said nothing, hoped that Bill would kill Vic with the knife. Chuck held Vic while Bill stabbed and killed him. On a charge of murdering Vic, Sam is

Question #1:_____

_____

Question #2:_____

_____

Question #3:_____

_____

19. Fifty-year-old Ginrus wrote to Collatera, his unemployed adult niece, and said: "If you come and live with me and take care of me and my property, Twin Oaks, for the rest of my life, I will leave Twin Oaks to you in my will." Collatera immediately moved in with Ginrus and took care of him and Twin Oaks until he was killed instantly in an automobile accident two weeks later. By his will, Ginrus left his entire estate, including Twin Oaks, to his unmarried sister, Sibling. Twin Oaks was reasonably worth $75,000. Assume that two days before Ginrus was killed, Collatera made an offer in writing to Drei to sell Twin Oaks to Drei for $75,000 when she should receive the property. Which of the following best states the rights of Collatera and Ginrus's estate (or Sibling)?

Question #1:_____

_____

Question #2:_____

_____

Question #3:_____

_____

20. Loyal, aged 60, who had no plans for early retirement, had worked for Mutate, Inc., for 20 years as a managerial employee-at-will when he had a conversation with the company's president, George Mutant, about Loyal's post-retirement goal of extensive travel around the United States. A month later, Mutant handed Loyal a written, signed resolution of the company's Board of Directors stating that when and if Loyal should decide to retire, at his option, the company, in recognition of his past service, would pay him a $2,000-per-month lifetime pension. (The company had no regularized retirement plan for

at-will employees.) Shortly thereafter, Loyal retired and immediately bought a $30,000 recreational vehicle for his planned travels. After receiving the promised $2,000 monthly pension from Mutate, Inc., for six months, Loyal, now unemployable elsewhere, received a letter from Mutate, Inc., advising him that the pension would cease immediately because of recessionary budget constraints affecting in varying degrees all managerial salaries and retirement pensions. In a suit against Mutate, Inc., for breach of contract, Loyal will probably

Question #1:_____

_____

Question #2:_____

_____

Question #3:_____

_____

D. Narrow Lens Exercise Answers

Note: The answers that follow are not exclusive; they are examples of questions resulting from active reading. You may have come up with others that are equally good. The point of the exercise is not getting the "right answer," but rather to develop your active reading skills.

1. Why does it matter that the death was accidental?
   Is this an issue of involuntary manslaughter?
   May larceny be committed against someone who is dead?
   Does it matter that nothing of value was taken?
   How does putting the money back into victim's pocket factor into whether a crime was committed?
   If this is a theft crime, has the taking and carrying away element been met?
2. What duty of care did Hospital owe Mom?
   Are hospital visitors invitees?
   Is there a difference between the emergency room and the rest of the hospital with respect to potential liability?
   Was the metal fixture apparent?
   Could the metal fixture have been made safer, or could a warning have been posted?

3. Does the common law or UCC apply?

Is there consideration for the option contract?

What legal detriment did Harriet suffer if she can revoke the offer at will?

Is the revocability clause in Harriet's offer valid?

Did Harriet's silence to Portia's comment about expected compensation constitute acceptance?

Does the fact that the offer was revoked the very next day factor into whether Reggie is obligated to pay?

Under what legal theory would Harriet be obligated to pay Norma?

4. Is the restriction on the power source valid?

What is the relevancy of the company only providing electricity to the development?

Does it matter whether or not the restriction was in the deed from Olm to Page?

Did Page have constructive notice of the covenant?

Does electricity "touch and concern" land?

5. Why does it matter that the statute is "generally applicable"?

Why are the purpose of the law and the consistency of enforcement important?

Why is it relevant that the Long's are "sincere"?

What is the test for evaluating the constitutionality of the statute?

Is the statute constitutional?

6. Is Wong's recorded statement hearsay?

If hearsay, is Wong's statement admissible?

How does Wong's wife factor in and why is she part of this question?

Are all the elements for the recorded recollection exception present?

7. Is Witness's statement being offered for its truth value or for some other reason?

What exception would be applicable, if hearsay?

Could the statement be excluded by definition from the Hearsay Rule?

How does the witness's refusal to testify factor into the hearsay analysis?

8. What type of manslaughter would this be, voluntary or involuntary?

How does the one year between the firing and the suicide factor in?

How is Martha's confession relevant?

Isn't there a causation problem here and couldn't there be other reasons that contributed to the suicide?

9. Is Guard's testimony about what the security director told him hearsay?

Why is it relevant that Guard no longer works for the store?

Does the former testimony exception apply here?

Is Guard's statement a party admission?

10. What are the property interests of joint tenants with right of survivorship?

Did Bob have a property interest to convey in 1950?

What is the state of title in 1970 when Bill died?

What is "marketable title" as opposed to just "title"?

11. Why is the testimony of the health department official about violations before and after the dinner relevant?

    Where is the evidence of actual causation?

    Why is the Restaurant the defendant — is this a respondeat superior issue?

    Could a jury draw an inference of negligence based on these facts?

    Couldn't one of the three subsequent meals have caused the infection?

    Would it be reasonable to conclude that Patron had an upset stomach as a result of the spicy food and then had a subsequent, unrelated upset stomach caused by bacteria in any one of the three meals he ate thereafter?

12. What type of forum is the auditorium?

    How does the fact that the discriminating group is private factor into the analysis?

    What test applies to determine whether the use of the auditorium is constitutional?

    Is there a content-neutral/viewpoint issue here?

13. Did Diane and Victor assume the risk of injury by consenting?

    Is pointing a loaded gun at someone without the intent to kill or injure "depraved heart/reckless indifference" or "gross negligence"?

    Was there a common law felony in the fact pattern?

14. Does the common law or UCC apply?

    Was the November 1 posting an offer?

    Does it matter that Student began performing before the November 1 posting?

    Was Student's written acceptance effective?

    Did Student accept by continuing to perform after he had knowledge of the November 1 posting?

    Does continued performance render the offer irrevocable, and if so, for how long?

15. What are the elements of an unjustifiable repudiation?

    Does Materboard have any rights after unjustifiably repudiating?

    Does the fact that Ram can buy more units than it can sell make it a lost volume seller?

    What damages are available to lost volume sellers?

16. Is the revocation provision in the licensing statute valid?

    Can the licensing board take action if the charges were dropped?

    What level of procedural due process is John entitled to with respect to the administrative board's hearing?

17. Can a state prohibit intestate succession to unacknowledged, illegitimate children?

    Is the government classifying illegitimate children based on whether or not they are acknowledged?

    If the government is classifying, is the class suspect or quasi-suspect?

    What level of scrutiny applies to illegitimacy?

18. Do onlookers have a legal obligation to act?

Is providing a knife without saying or doing anything else enough for accomplice liability?

Is mere encouragement enough for accomplice liability?

Is intent to kill without any affirmative act or encouragement enough for accomplice liability?

19. Has a valid contract been formed between Collatera and Ginrus?

Where is the consideration in the agreement between Collatera and Ginrus?

Is Collatera's offer to Drei valid?

What effect does Ginrus's death have on the outstanding offer Collatera made to Drei?

20. Is recognition for past service valid consideration?

Why is it relevant that there is no regular retirement plan for at-will employees?

What effect does the making of six payments have on the validity of the contract?

If the contract is unenforceable at law, did Loyal justifiably rely on Mutant's promise to his detriment?

Chapter 4

Active Learning
for the MBE

The exercises in Chapter 2 were designed to stimulate active thought as you read through fact patterns. The ability to *answer* questions raised by active thinking is fundamental to success on the bar exam. In the previous chapter, our focus was on identifying questions; in this chapter, we move farther on in the active learning process by answering questions that resulted from active reading. This process of actively studying for the bar exam is critically important because simultaneously you will be reviewing/learning substantive law and developing analytical and writing skills.

The two examples that follow demonstrate how we are building on the narrow lens concept. First, I ask questions as I read. Then, I go one step further by answering the questions raised by active reading. With practice and over time, you will be able to increase your analytical speed and accuracy in asking relevant questions and quickly providing answers either in your head or by jotting notes in the margins.

A. Active Learning Example I

Sand Company operated an installation for distributing sand and gravel. The installation was adjacent to a residential area. On Sand's grounds there was a chute with polished metal sides for loading sand and gravel into trucks. The trucks being loaded stopped on the public street below the chute. After closing hours, a plywood screen was placed in the chute and the ladder used for inspection was removed to another section of the installation. For several months, however, a number of children, 8 to 10 years of age, had been playing on Sand's property and the adjoining street after closing hours. The children found the ladder and also discovered that they could remove the plywood screen from the chute and slide down to the street below. Sand knew of this activity. One evening, the children were using the chute as a play device. As an automobile driven by Commuter approached the chute, Ladd, an 8-year-old boy, slid down just in front of the automobile. Commuter applied her brakes, but they suddenly failed, and she hit and injured Ladd. Commuter saw the child in time to have avoided hitting him if her brakes had worked properly. Two days previously, Commuter had taken her car to Garage to have her brakes inspected. Garage inspected the brakes and told her that the brakes were in perfect working order. Claims were asserted on behalf of Ladd by his proper legal representative against Sand, Commuter, and Garage. On Ladd's claim against Sand, will Ladd prevail?

> *Comment:* The first question I asked myself is why the bar examiners told me the children's ages because whenever I see numbers, I know they are almost always important. A different standard of care applies to property owners when children are involved. I know the general rule is that property owners owe no duty of care to trespassers, except they may not intentionally injure them. But there is a rule modification when it comes to children: A property owner has a duty to exercise reasonable care regarding artificial conditions, also known as "attractive nuisances," posing a threat to a child's safety. Then, we are told that Sand knew of the children's activities, which leads to the question of what effect this has on his potential liability. Once Sand is on notice, it has an affirmative duty to take reasonable care to prevent a trespassing child from injury. Lastly, we are told that the brakes failed after they were inspected. Why does that matter? Garage has a duty to protect foreseeable plaintiffs from foreseeable harm. It is foreseeable that a child playing on a public street would be injured as a result of negligently inspected brakes.

B. Active Learning Example II

Defendant became intoxicated at a bar. He got into his car and drove away. Within a few blocks, craving another drink, he stopped his car in the middle of the street, picked up a brick, and broke the display window of a liquor store. As he was reaching for a bottle, the night watchman arrived. Startled, Defendant turned and struck the watchman on the head with the bottle, killing him. At Defendant's trial for the murder of the watchman, the court should in substance charge the jury on the issue of the defense of intoxication that

> *Comment:* The first sentence leads to the question of what effect intoxication has on liability. Voluntary intoxication is not an excuse for committing a crime. It may, however, negate the intent element for specific intent crimes. If a criminal defendant lacked the capacity to form the specific intent for the crime in question, voluntary intoxication may be raised as an affirmative defense. Voluntary

intoxication is not a defense for general intent crimes. The next question is whether a crime was committed when Defendant broke the window of the store. We know Defendant intended to steal a bottle of liquor. So we have intent and a breaking, which raises a burglary issue that I can discount under common law analysis because a liquor store is not a dwelling. Lastly, there's a killing so I need to determine whether or not this is common law murder. I can't tell from the facts whether there is an intent to kill, but I'm reasonably certain that hitting someone on the head with a bottle is evidence of an intent to cause serious bodily injury or, perhaps, of depraved indifference. Remember that common law murder is the unlawful killing of a person with malice aforethought. Malice aforethought may be shown by: (1) an intent to kill, (2) an intent to cause serious bodily injury, (3) depraved indifference, or (4) felony murder.

C. Active Learning Exercises

In the fact patterns that follow, read through the entire scenario first using your broad lens. Use reference materials for help with the substantive law. As you move forward with your bar preparation, you will become more skilled and faster in asking (the subject of Chapter 3) and answering (the subject of this chapter) relevant questions while you read. Here, you are prompted with the questions you will learn to ask and answer yourself with dedicated and focused practice before you begin your commercial bar review course. By studying in this fashion, you are learning substantive law in the context of fact patterns, which is much more effective than memorizing law from outlines without any context.

1. On May 1, Ohner telegraphed Byer, "Will sell you any or all of the lots in Grover subdivision at $5,000 each? Details follow in letter." The letter contained all the necessary details concerning terms of payment, insurance, mortgages, etc., and provided, "This offer remains open until June 1." On May 2, after the investor had received the telegram but before he had received the letter, Byer telegraphed Ohner, "Accept your offer with respect to lot 101." Both parties knew that there were 50 lots in the Grove subdivision and that they were numbered 101 through 150. On May 3, Ohner telephoned Byer, saying that because he had just discovered that a shopping center was going to be erected adjacent to the Grove subdivision, he would "have to have $6,000 for each of the lots including lot 101." During the telephone call, Byer agreed to pay him $6,000 for lot 101. On May 6, Byer telegraphed, "Accept your offer with respect to the rest of the lots." Assuming that the two contracts were formed and that there is no controlling statute, Byer will most likely be required to pay

The common law of contracts applies because

> *Reminder:* The first issue in any contracts question is whether the UCC or the common law applies.

_____

_____

Is the option valid? Would your answer be different under the UCC?

_____

_____

_____

_____

After accepting the offer for lot 101, does Byer still have the power to accept the offer for the remaining lots?

_____

_____

_____

_____

Is the contract modification for lot 101 valid? Would your answer be different under the UCC?

_____

_____

_____

_____

What effect does the May 3 communication have on the rest of the lots?

_____

_____

_____

_____

What are the terms of the two contracts?

_____

_____

_____

_____

2. A vacant lot is contiguous to a farm. Thirty years ago, the then-record owner of the vacant lot executed and delivered to the owner of the farm an instrument in writing that was denominated "Deed of Conveyance," granting the farmer and her heirs and assigns a right-of-way for egress and ingress to the farm. If the quoted provision was sufficient to create an interest in land, the instrument met all other requirements for a valid grant. The farmer held record title in fee simple to the farm. Twelve years ago, an investor succeeded to the vacant lot owner's title in fee simple in the vacant lot and seven years ago the farmer's daughter succeeded to the farmer's title in fee simple in the farm by a deed, which made no mention of a right-of-way or driveway. At the time the farmer's daughter took title, there existed, across the vacant lot, a driveway that showed evidence that it had been used regularly to travel between a highway and the farm. The farm did have frontage on another public road, but this means of access was seldom used because it was not as convenient to the dwelling situated on the farm as was the highway. The driveway was originally established by the farmer. The farmer's daughter has regularly used the driveway since acquiring title. The period of time required to acquire rights by prescription in the jurisdiction is ten years. Six months ago the investor notified the farmer's daughter that he planned to develop a portion of the vacant lot as a

residential subdivision and that she should cease any use of the driveway. After some negotiations, the investor offered to permit the farmer's daughter to construct another driveway to connect with the streets of the proposed subdivision. She declined this offer on the ground that travel from the lot to the main road would be more circuitous. The farmer's daughter brought an appropriate action against the investor to obtain a definitive adjudication of their respective rights. In such lawsuit the investor relied upon the defense that the location of the easement created by the grant was governed by reasonableness and that the investor's proposed solution was reasonable. The investor's defense should

What kind of property interest was granted to the farmer?

> *Reminder:* Whenever you see a property conveyance, define the present estate and future interest created.

_____

_____

What kind of interest does the investor hold in the vacant lot?

_____

_____

_____

Define the property interests after the farmer's daughter acquires title to the farm.

_____

_____

_____

_____

The location of an easement is usually determined by the grantor, the holder of the servient tenement. Does it matter that the easement was established by the holder of the dominant tenement?

_____

_____

_____

_____

Is there an adverse possession issue here?

_____

_____

_____

_____

Does the farmer's daughter have to cease using the driveway?

_____

_____

_____

_____

Does the farmer's daughter have an obligation to accept the investor's offer?

_____

_____

_____

_____

Is the location of the easement in fact governed by reasonableness?

_____

_____

_____

_____

3. An ordinance of City makes it unlawful to park a motor vehicle on a City street within ten feet of a fire hydrant. At 1:55 p.m. Parker, realizing he must be in Bank before it closed at 2:00 p.m. and finding no other space available, parked his automobile in front of a fire hydrant on a City street. Parker then hurried into the bank, leaving his aged neighbor, Ned, as a passenger in the rear seat of the car. About five minutes later, and while Parker was still in Bank, Driver was driving down the street. Driver swerved to avoid what he mistakenly thought was a hole in the street and sideswiped Parker's car. Parker's car was turned over on top of the hydrant, breaking the hydrant and causing a small flood of water. Parker's car was severely damaged and Ned was badly injured. There is no applicable guest statute. If Parker asserts a claim against Driver for damage to Parker's automobile, the most likely result is that Parker will

What is the purpose of this ordinance?

_____

_____

Is Parker negligent per se with respect to Ned for parking in front of the hydrant?

_____

_____

_____

_____

What duty of care did Parker owe Ned?

_____

_____

_____

_____

Was Driver negligent?

_____

_____

_____

_____

What is a guest statute?

_____

_____

_____

_____

4. Ames had painted Bell's house under a contract that called for payment of $2,000. Bell, contending in good faith that the porch had not been painted properly, refused to pay anything. On June 15, Ames mailed a letter to Bell stating, "I am in serious need of money. Please send the $2,000 to me before July 1." On June 18, Bell replied, "I will settle for $1,800 provided you agree to repaint the porch." Ames did not reply to this letter. Thereafter, Bell mailed a check for $1,800 marked, "Payment in full on the Ames-Bell painting contract as per letter dated June 18." Ames received the check on June 30. Because he was badly in need of money, Ames cashed the check without objection and spent the

proceeds but has refused to repaint the porch. Bell's refusal to pay anything to Ames when he finished painting was a

Does the UCC or common law apply?

_____

_____

What type of agreement did Bell propose on June 18?

_____

_____

_____

_____

Does Ames's silence constitute acceptance?

_____

_____

_____

_____

What is the effect of Ames's cashing the check but refusing to repaint?

_____

_____

_____

_____

5. Passer was driving his pickup truck along a lonely road on a very cold night. Passer saw Tom, who was a stranger, lying in a field by the side of the road and apparently injured. Passer stopped his truck, alighted, and, upon examining Tom, discovered that Tom was intoxicated and in danger of suffering from exposure to the cold. However, Passer returned to his truck and drove away without making any effort to help Tom. Tom remained lying at the same place and was later injured when a car driven by Traveler, who was drowsy and inattentive, veered off the road into the field and hit Tom. Traveler did not see Tom prior to hitting him. If Tom asserts a claim against Passer for damages for his injuries, will Tom prevail?

Does Passer owe Tom a duty of care?

Why is it relevant that Tom is a stranger?

When Passer examined Tom and determined that Tom was drunk and his life was at risk due to the extreme cold, did he then have a duty to Tom?

_____

_____

6. John Doe, the owner of a milk container manufacturing firm, sought to
focus public attention on the milk packaging law of the State of Clinton
in order to have it repealed. On a weekday at 12:00 p.m., he delivered an
excited, animated, and loud harangue on the steps of the State Capitol in
front of the main entryway. An audience of 200 onlookers, who gathered
on the steps, heckled him and laughed as he delivered his tirade. Doe
repeatedly stated, gesturing expressively and making faces, that "the
g-ddamned milk packaging law is stupid," and that "I will strangle
every one of those g-ddamned legislators I can get hold of because
this law they created proves they are all too dumb to live." After
about 15 minutes, Doe stopped speaking, and the amused crowd dispersed. The relevant statute of the State of Clinton prohibits "all speech
making, picketing, and public gatherings of every sort on the Capitol
steps in front of the main entryway between 7:45 a.m.-8:15 a.m., 11:45
a.m.-12:15 p.m., 12:45 p.m.-1:15 p.m., and 4:45 p.m.-5:15 p.m., on Capitol working days." If Doe is prosecuted under the "Capitol steps" statute
and defends on constitutional grounds, which of the following best
describes the proper burden of proof?

Are the steps of the building a "public forum"? Explain.

_____

_____

_____

_____

Is "I will strangle . . ." protected speech?

_____

_____

_____

_____

What is the significance of the audience's laughter?

_____

_____

_____

_____

Is this regulation content-based or content-neutral?

_____

_____

_____

_____

Under what level of constitutional scrutiny should the law be analyzed?

_____

_____

_____

_____

7. Sam decided to kill his boss, Anna, after she told him that he would be fired if his work did not improve. Sam knew Anna was scheduled to go on a business trip on Monday morning. On Sunday morning, Sam went to the company parking garage and put a bomb in the company car that Anna usually drove. The bomb was wired to go off when the car engine started. Sam then left town. At 5:00 a.m. on Monday, Sam, after driving all night, was overcome with remorse and had a change of heart. He called the security officer on duty at the company and told him about the bomb. The security officer said he would take care

of the matter. An hour later, the officer put a note on Anna's desk telling her of the message. He then looked at the car but could not see any signs of a bomb. He printed a sign saying "DO NOT USE THIS CAR," put it on the windshield, and went to call the police. Before the police arrived, Lois, a company vice president, got into the car and started the engine. The bomb went off, killing her. The jurisdiction defines murder in the first degree as any homicide committed with premeditation and deliberation or any murder in the commission of a common law felony. Second-degree murder is defined as all other murder at common law. Manslaughter is defined by the common law. Sam is guilty of

Does Sam's change of heart effectively negate his intent to kill Anna?

_____

_____

_____

_____

What effect, if any, does the officer's note and sign have on whether Sam committed a crime?

_____

_____

_____

_____

Sam did not intend to kill Lois — what issue does Lois's death raise?

_____

_____

_____

_____

8. Ortega owned Blackacre in fee simple and by his will specifically devised Blackacre as follows: "To my daughter, Eugenia, her heirs and assigns, but if Eugenia dies survived by a husband and a child or children, then to Eugenia's husband during his lifetime with remainder to Eugenia's children, their heirs and assigns. Specifically provided, however, that if Eugenia dies survived by a husband and no child, Blackacre is specifically devised to my nephew, Luis, his heirs and assigns." While Ortega's will was in probate, Luis quitclaimed all interest in Blackacre to Eugenia's husband, Jose. Three years later, Eugenia died, survived by Jose but no children. Eugenia left a will devising her interest in Blackacre to Jose. The only applicable statute provides that any interest in land is freely alienable. Luis instituted an appropriate action against Jose to establish title to Blackacre. Judgment should be for

What type of future interest does the will create for Luis?

_____

_____

_____

_____

What is a quitclaim deed?

_____

_____

_____

_____

What type of interest does the will create for Eugenia?

_____

_____

What type of interest do Eugenia's heirs have?

9. A city ordinance requires a taxicab operator's license to operate a taxicab in King City. The ordinance states that the sole criteria for the issuance of such a license are driving ability and knowledge of the geography of King City. An applicant is tested by the city for these qualifications with a detailed questionnaire, written and oral examinations, and a practical behind-the-wheel examination. The ordinance does not limit the number of licenses that may be issued. It does, however, allow any citizen to file an objection to the issuance of a particular license, but only on the ground that an applicant does not possess the required qualifications. City licensing officials are also authorized by the ordinance to determine, in their discretion, whether to hold an evidentiary hearing on an objection before issuing a license. Sandy applies for a taxicab operator's license and is found to be fully qualified after completing the usual licensing process. Her name is then posted as a prospective licensee, subject only to the objection process. John, a licensed taxicab driver, files an objection to the issuance of such a license to Sandy solely on the ground that the grant of a license to Sandy would impair the value of John's existing license. John demands a hearing before a license is issued to Sandy so that he may have an opportunity to prove his claim. City licensing officials refuse to hold such a hearing, and they issue a license to Sandy. John petitions for review of this action by city officials in an appropriate court, alleging that the Constitution requires city licensing officials to grant his request for a hearing before issuing a license to Sandy. In this case, the court should rule for

Is Fourteenth Amendment Due Process triggered when the government adversely affects one's property interest?

_____

_____

_____

_____

John has no right to a hearing because . . .

_____

_____

_____

10. Astin left her car at Garrison's Garage to have repair work done. After completing the repairs, Garrison took the car out for a test drive and was involved in an accident that caused damages to Placek. A statute imposes liability on the owner of an automobile for injuries to a third party that are caused by the negligence of any person driving the automobile with the owner's consent. The statute applies to situations of this kind, even if the owner did not specifically authorize the mechanic to test-drive the car. Placek sued Astin and Garrison jointly for damages arising from the accident. In that action, Astin cross-claims to recover from Garrison the amount of any payment Astin may be required to make to Placek. The trier of fact has determined that the accident was caused solely by negligent driving on Garrison's part, and that Placek's damages were $100,000. In this action, the proper outcome will be that

Why doesn't joint and several liability apply to these facts?

_____

_____

_____

_____

What are the doctrines of contribution and indemnification?

_____

_____

_____

_____

11. In a jurisdiction that has abolished the felony murder rule, but otherwise follows the common law of murder, Sally and Ralph, both armed with automatic weapons, went into a bank to rob it. Ralph ordered all the persons in the bank to lie on the floor. When some were slow to obey, Sally, not intending to hit anyone, fired about 15 rounds into the air. One of these ricocheted off a stone column and struck and killed a customer in the bank. Sally and Ralph were charged with murder of the customer. Which of the following is correct?

What is the felony murder rule?

_____

_____

_____

_____

What are the elements of accomplice liability?

_____

_____

12. On December 15, Lawyer received from Stationer, Inc., a retailer of office supplies, an offer consisting of its catalog and a signed letter stating, "We will supply you with as many of the items in the enclosed catalog as you order during the next calendar year. We assure you that this offer and the prices in the catalog will remain firm throughout the coming year." Assume that no other correspondence passed between Stationer and Lawyer until the following April 15 (four months later), when Stationer received from Lawyer a faxed order for "100 reams of your paper, catalog item #101." Did Lawyer's April 15 fax constitute an effective acceptance of Stationer's offer at the prices specified in the catalog?

Is the option valid?

_____

_____

_____

_____

Would your answer be different under common law analysis?

_____

_____

_____

_____

Why is the passage of four months relevant?

_____

_____

_____

_____

13. Plaintiff sued Defendant for injuries sustained in an automobile collision. During Plaintiff's hospital stay, Doctor, a staff physician, examined Plaintiff's X rays and said to Plaintiff, "You have a fracture of two vertebrae, C4 and C5." Intern, who was accompanying Doctor on her rounds, immediately wrote the diagnosis on Plaintiff's hospital record. At trial, the hospital records custodian testifies that Plaintiff's hospital record was made and kept in the ordinary course of the hospital's business. The entry reporting Doctor's diagnosis is

What is hearsay within hearsay?

_____

_____

_____

_____

What are the two instances of hearsay in this fact pattern?

_____

_____

_____

_____

Why is it relevant that the Plaintiff's record was made and kept in the "ordinary course of business"?

_____

_____

_____

_____

14. David is being tried in federal court for criminal conspiracy with John to violate federal narcotics law. At trial, the prosecutor calls David's new wife, Wanda, and asks her to testify about a meeting between David and John that she observed before she married David. Which of the following is the most accurate statement of the applicable rule concerning whether Wanda may testify?

The two testimonial privileges related to marriage are . . .

_____

_____

_____

_____

Why is it relevant that the conversation between David and John occurred before Wanda married David and not after?

_____

_____

_____

_____

15. Water District is an independent municipal water-supply district incorporated under the applicable laws of the state of Green. The district was created solely to supply water to an entirely new community in a recently developed area of Green. That new community is racially, ethnically, and socioeconomically diverse, and the community has never engaged in any discrimination against members of minority groups. The five-member, elected governing board of the newly created Water District contains two persons who are members of racial minority groups. At its first meeting, the governing board of Water District adopted a rule unqualifiedly setting aside 25 percent of all positions on the staff of the District and 25 percent of all contracts to be awarded by the District to members of racial minority groups. The purpose of the rule was "to help redress the historical discrimination against these groups in this country and to help them achieve economic parity with other groups in our society." Assume that no federal statute applies. A suit by appropriate parties challenges the constitutionality of these set-asides. In this suit, the most appropriate ruling on the basis of applicable United States Supreme Court precedent would be that the set-asides are

What are the "suspect classes"?

_____

_____

_____

_____

What is the constitutional test that applies to race-based classifications?

_____

_____

_____

_____

Are set-asides ever constitutional?

_____

_____

_____

_____

16. Carr ran into and injured Pedersen, a pedestrian. With Carr in his car were Wanda and Walter Passenger. Passerby saw the accident and called the police department, which sent Sheriff to investigate. All of these people were available as potential witnesses in the case of *Pedersen v. Carr*. Pedersen alleges that Carr, while drunk, struck Pedersen who was in a duly marked crosswalk. Pedersen's counsel wants to introduce testimony of Sheriff that at the police station Carr told Sheriff, "I think this was probably my fault." The trial judge should rule this testimony

Why is Carr's statement hearsay?

_____

_____

_____

_____

Even though hearsay, the Sheriff's testimony is admissible because . . .

_____

_____

_____

_____

17. [Same fact pattern as the previous question.] Pedersen's counsel wants to have Sheriff testify to the following statement made to him by Walter Passenger, out of the presence of Carr: "We were returning from a party at which we had all been drinking." The trial judge should rule this testimony

The statement in question #16 is admissible, but the statement here is inadmissible. Why? What's the critical distinction between these two questions?

_____

_____

_____

_____

18. Maria is the owner and possessor of Goodacre, on which there is a lumber yard. Maria conveyed to Reliable Electric Company the right to construct and use an overhead electric line across Goodacre to serve other properties. The conveyance was in writing, but the writing made no provision concerning the responsibility for repair or maintenance of the line. Reliable installed the poles and erected the electric line in a proper and workmanlike manner. Neither Maria nor Reliable took any steps toward the maintenance or repair of the line after it was built. Neither party complained to the other about any failure to repair. Because of the failure to repair or properly maintain the line, it fell to the ground during a storm. In doing so, it caused a fire in the lumber yard and did considerable damage. Maria sued Reliable Electric Company to recover for damages to the lumber yard. The decision should be for

What type of property interest did Maria grant Reliable?

_____

_____

_____

_____

Which party had the duty to maintain the electric line?

_____

_____

_____

_____

19. Acorp and Beeco are companies that each manufacture pesticide X. Their manufacturing plants are located along the same river. During a specific 24-hour period, each plant discharged pesticide into the river. Both plants were operated negligently and such negligence caused the discharge of the pesticide into the river. Landesmann operated a cattle ranch downstream from the plants of Acorp and Beeco. Landesmann's cattle drank from the river and were poisoned by the pesticide. The amount of the discharge from either plant alone would not have been sufficient to cause any harm to Landesmann's cattle. If Landesmann asserts a claim against Acorp and Beeco, what, if anything, will Landesmann recover?

What are the tests for actual causation?

_____

_____

_____

_____

Which actual causation test applies to these facts?

_____

_____

_____

_____

20. The vintner of a large vineyard offers balloon rides to visitors who wish to tour the grounds from the air. During one of the rides, the vintner was forced to make a crash landing on his own property. Without the vintner's knowledge or consent, a trespasser had entered the vineyard to camp for a couple of days. The trespasser was injured when he was hit by the basket of the descending balloon. If the trespasser sues the vintner to recover damages for his injuries, will the trespasser prevail?

What is the duty of care owed to unknown trespassers?

_____

_____

What is the duty of care owed to discovered trespassers?

_____

_____

D. Active Learning Exercise Answers

Question 1

The common law of contracts applies because . . .
This contract is for the sale of real property rather than a good.
Is the option valid? Would your answer be different under the UCC?
No, option contracts require consideration at common law. Yes, because options do not require consideration under the UCC if the offer is signed for the time stated or, in the absence of a specified time, no longer than three months.
After accepting the offer for lot 101, does Buyer still have the power to accept the offer for the remaining lots?
The acceptance with respect to lot 101 probably terminates the power of acceptance for the remaining lots unless there is consideration for the option. Under the common law, the power of acceptance terminates after a reasonable period, but in no case may the offer remain open until June 1.
Is the contract modification for lot 101 valid? Would your answer be different under the UCC?

No, contract modifications require consideration at common law. The modification would be valid under the UCC as long as it was made in good faith and Byer agreed.

What effect does the May 3 communication have on the rest of the lots?
When Buyer asks for $6,000 for the remaining lots, this isn't an attempt to modify because there isn't an existing contract for those lots. This is an offer to sell each or all of the remaining lots at $6,000 per lot and removes any doubt that the power to accept these lots at $5,000 each has terminated because, even if that offer remained open as of May 3, the communication that day served as a revocation and new offer.

What are the terms of the two contracts?
The first contract is for the sale of lot 101 for $5,000. The modification of price was not valid due to lack of consideration. The second contract was for the sale of lots 102-150 at $6,000 each because the $5,000 offer explicitly terminated with the revocation and new offer on May 3. The option to keep the offer open at $5,000 was not valid without consideration at common law.

Question 2

What kind of property interest was granted to the farmer?
The then-record owner of the vacant lot granted an express easement for access to the farm.

What kind of interest does the vacant lot owner hold?
The vacant lot owner holds title in fee simple, subject to the easement.

Define the property interests after the farmer's daughter acquires title.
The farmer's daughter holds fee simple title to the farm. The easement is still valid because it runs with the land, by definition, and by the terms of the original deed.

The location of an easement is usually determined by the grantor, the holder of the servient tenement. Does it matter that the easement was established by the holder of the dominant tenement?
The fact that the easement was established by the farmer should pose no problem. Presumably the vacant lot owner, as the holder of the servient tenement, could have established it but didn't, and there is no indication in the facts that he objected to the location.

Is there an adverse possession issue here?
Regular use of the driveway removes any issue of extinction of the easement. The mention of "prescription" triggers adverse possession of the easement, but that doesn't appear to be an issue thus far.

Does the farmer's daughter have to cease using the driveway?
No, she holds a valid easement, which isn't extinguished because the lot owner wants to use his property differently.

Does the farmer's daughter have an obligation to accept lot owner's offer?
As the holder of a valid property interest, she is under no obligation to accept the offer, no matter how reasonable.
Is the location of the easement in fact governed by reasonableness?
The location was established by the farmer and at least implicitly acquiesced to by the owner of the vacant lot. The reasonableness of the proposal is irrelevant.

Question 3

What is the purpose of this ordinance?
The purpose of the ordinance is to allow firefighters access to the hydrant in the event of a fire.
Is Parker negligent per se with respect to Ned for parking in front of the hydrant?
Parker isn't negligent per se because Ned isn't part of the class of people intended to be protected by the ordinance. Under traditional negligence, even if Parker failed to exercise reasonable care by parking in front of the hydrant, that failure did not cause Ned's injuries because it is not foreseeable that a car would flip over on a hydrant.
What duty of care did Parker owe Ned?
Parker owed Ned a duty to use the degree of care a reasonably prudent person would exercise in the same or similar situation.
Was Driver negligent?
Yes, Driver probably failed in his duty to exercise reasonable care by swerving because there wasn't a pothole to avoid.
What is a guest statute?
A guest statute limits the liability a driver owes to nonpaying passengers.

Question 4

Does the UCC or common law apply?
The common law applies because this is a service contract.
What type of agreement did Bell propose on June 18?
Bell's proposal is for an accord and satisfaction, which is an agreement for substitute performance. The accord is the new agreement and the performance is the satisfaction. The dispute in good faith serves as new consideration for the agreement.
Does Ames's silence constitute acceptance?
No, the general rule is acceptance requires some affirmative act by the offeree.
What is the effect of Ames's cashing the check but refusing to repaint?
When Ames cashed the check, he accepted the accord. The refusal to perform (to paint) constitutes a breach of contract.

Question 5

Does Passer owe Tom a duty of care?
No, there is no duty to rescue someone in peril absent a special relationship.
Why is it relevant that Tom is a stranger?
Tom would have a duty to render assistance if one of the instances of a special relationship (for example, parent/child) were present.
When Passer examined Tom and determined that Tom was drunk and his life was at risk due to the extreme cold, did he then have a duty to Tom?
No, as long as Passer didn't make Tom's condition worse.

Question 6

Are the steps of the building a "public forum"?
Yes, because steps in front of a building where law making occurs are traditionally viewed as a public forum.
Is "I will strangle . . ." protected speech?
Yes, on these facts the law is probably valid but may not be applied to Doe. Under the *Brandenburg* "clear and present danger" test, "I will strangle . . ." is probably not intended to produce imminent unlawful behavior.
What is the significance of the audience's laughter?
The laughter goes to the second prong of the *Brandenburg* test: Laughing implies that the crowd does not take Doe seriously. If the crowd does not take Doe seriously, it is unlikely that Doe will in fact incite imminent unlawful conduct.
Is this regulation content-based or content-neutral?
It is a content-neutral time, place, manner restriction.
Under what level of constitutional scrutiny should the law be analyzed?
Time, place, manner restrictions are analyzed under quasi-intermediate or intermediate-plus scrutiny. The law must be substantially related to an important government objective and leave open alternative means of communication.

Question 7

Does Sam's change of heart effectively negate his intent to kill Anna?
No, because Sam acted with the intent to kill. That he no longer had the intent to kill at the time of the result of his act is irrelevant and does not negate his intent.
What effect, if any, does the officer's note and sign have on whether Sam committed a crime?
The security officer is a red herring who has nothing to do with Sam's criminal culpability because Sam acted with the intent to kill.

Sam did not intend to kill Lois — what issue does Lois's death raise?
Lois's death raises the issue of transferred intent. Under the doctrine of transferred intent, the fact that an unintended victim suffered the harm intended for someone else does not absolve a criminal defendant of culpability. The intent and act are transferred from the intended victim to the unintended victim.

Question 8

What type of future interest does the will create for Luis?
Luis has a contingent remainder in fee simple. The remainder is contingent upon Eugenia dying with a husband, but without issue.
What is a quitclaim deed?
A transfer of whatever property interest a transferor has to a transferee that contains no warranty regarding the state of the title.
What type of interest does the will create for Eugenia?
Eugenia holds title in fee simple.
What type of interest do Eugenia's heirs have?
Eugenia's heirs have no property interest whatsoever. If Eugenia has a child, that child holds a vested remainder subject to open (the firstborn child is certain to take, but the extent of his/her interest is undetermined because Eugenia may have more children).

Question 9

Is Fourteenth Amendment Due Process triggered when the government adversely affects one's interest?
No, an adverse impact is not enough to trigger procedural due process. One must be deprived of life, liberty, or property before the right to some kind of hearing attaches.
John has no right to a hearing because ...
The government is not depriving John of life, liberty, or property.

Question 10

Why doesn't joint and several liability apply to these facts?
Astin wasn't negligent. Joint and several liability applies when two or more tortfeasors are negligent. In that case, a plaintiff may recover the entire amount of her damages from any one of the tortfeasors.
What are the doctrines of contribution and indemnification?
Under the doctrine of contribution, a tortfeasor who pays more than her pro rata share of damages has the right to seek reimbursement from the other tortfeasors for the amount she paid over her share. Indemnification refers to the situation where one who has been held liable, but is not at fault, may

recover all damages she has paid from the other tortfeasors, which is the situation here. The most common example of indemnification occurs in the employer/employee vicarious liability context. An employer held vicariously liable for the tort of his employee may recover from that employee any payment the employer made in satisfaction of the judgment.

Question 11

What is the felony murder rule?
At common law, the death of a person while defendant is committing an inherently dangerous felony is common law murder.
What are the elements of accomplice liability?
Intent that a crime be committed plus some affirmative act or aid in furtherance of the crime.

Question 12

Is the option valid?
No, because under the UCC, an option lasting longer than three months requires consideration. Here, there is no consideration for the option contract.
Would your answer be different under common law analysis?
No, under the common law, the option would not be valid for any length of time without consideration.
Why is the passage of four months relevant?
The offer was irrevocable for three months; after that, Stationer could revoke because the option contract was no longer valid without consideration. Stationer did not revoke the offer, so on April 15, the offer was still open and the acceptance is valid. The passage of three months only applies to the irrevocability of the offer; it does not terminate the power of the offeree to accept thereafter.

Question 13

What is hearsay within hearsay?
A hearsay statement that contains another hearsay statement. A common example is a report that memorializes someone else's out of court statement.
What are the two instances of hearsay in this fact pattern?
The doctor's statement and the intern's recording of the doctor's statement.
Why is it relevant that the plaintiff's record was made and kept in the "ordinary course of business"?
In order for the hearsay records exception to apply, the record must be of the kind that is regularly made in the course of that business.

Question 14

The two testimonial privileges related to marriage are ...
(1) The marital communications privilege, which protects confidential communications between husband and wife (and belongs to both), and (2) the marital testimonial privilege, which prevents one spouse from being compelled to testify against the other. The testimonial privilege belongs only to the witness spouse; the defendant spouse cannot prevent a willing witness spouse from testifying.
Why is it relevant that the conversation between David and Jon occurred before Wanda married David and not after?
At common law, the testimonial privilege does not apply to events taking place before the marriage.

Question 15

What are the "suspect classes"?
The suspect classifications for Equal Protection analysis are: race, religion, national origin, and alienage. (There is an exception for aliens performing "government functions"; such restrictions are analyzed under the rational basis test.)
What is the constitutional test that applies to race-based classifications?
Race-based classifications are presumptively unconstitutional and subject to strict scrutiny. The government has the burden of proving the classification is necessary in order to achieve a compelling governmental interest.
Are set-asides ever constitutional?
Yes, if the set-aside is necessary to remedy actual discrimination.

Question 16

Why is Carr's statement hearsay?
The statement is hearsay because it was made out of court and is being offered for the truth of the matter asserted therein — that the accident was Carr's fault.
Even though hearsay, the Sheriff's testimony is admissible because ...
Carr's statement is considered a party admission. A party admission is a statement made by a party to a lawsuit offered against that party. The rule is that such statements are admissible, despite being offered for their truth value, and are therefore considered nonhearsay.

Question 17

The statement in question #16 is admissible, but the statement here is inadmissible. Why? What's the critical distinction between these two questions?

The statement, "We were returning from a party at which we had all been drinking," is inadmissible hearsay because the passenger is not a party to the lawsuit, so the party admission exemption is inapplicable to these facts.

Question 18

What type of property interest did Maria grant Reliable?

Reliable possesses an express easement in gross.

Which party had the duty to maintain the electric line?

The rule is the dominant estate holder, Reliable, has the duty to maintain the easement.

Question 19

What are the tests for actual causation?

Normally, the "but for" test is used to establish actual causation. If it can be said that "but for the defendant's negligent act, the plaintiff would not have been injured," actual causation is established. However, when two sources of negligent conduct combine to cause injury and neither one can meet the "but for" test, a court will apply the substantial factor test. Under the substantial factor test, the actual causation requirement will be met if a defendant materially contributed to plaintiff's injury.

Which actual causation test applies to these facts?

Since both defendants were negligent, the substantial factor test applies.

Question 20

What is the duty of care owed to unknown trespassers?

There is no duty of care to unknown trespassers. A property owner is not liable to unknown trespassers for failing to use reasonable care in maintaining his land or keeping his premises safe.

What is the duty of care owed to discovered trespassers?

Generally speaking, the duty owed to discovered trespassers is reasonable care. A property owner must warn of artificial conditions or hidden dangers that may cause serious injury or death.

Chapter 5

The Capstone: Learning Through Wrong Answers

In the preface, I mentioned that the best way to learn, remember, and, most importantly, apply the law for the bar exam is through wrong answers in the context of fact patterns — that is, learning from mistakes. In this chapter, I have selected questions used in my class where *more students selected the same wrong answer* than the correct answer choice as a way of highlighting some important concepts and common errors you can avoid. For each question, I have indicated that wrong answer. See if you can articulate the error my students made and then select the correct answer. Provide a concise rationale for your choice. By doing so, you will be actively learning while simultaneously honing your essay writing skills. If you can identify the mistakes my students made, the reason for the mistake, and the right answer, you will be well on your way to bar exam success and ready to begin your commercial course.

A. Learning Through a *Wrong* Answer Example I

A state statute divides murder into degrees. First-degree murder is defined as murder with premeditation and deliberation or a homicide in the commission of arson, rape, robbery, burglary, or kidnapping. Second-degree murder is all other murder at common law. In which of the following situations is Defendant most likely to be guilty of first-degree murder?

   (A) Immediately after being insulted by Robert, Defendant takes a knife and stabs and kills Robert.
   (B) Angered over having been struck by Sam, Defendant buys rat poison and puts it in Sam's coffee. Sam drinks the coffee and dies as a result.
   (C) Intending to injure Fred, Defendant lies in wait and, as Fred comes by, Defendant strikes him with a broom handle. As a result of the blow, Fred dies.

(D) Defendant, highly intoxicated, discovers a revolver on a table. He picks it up, points it at Alice, and pulls the trigger. The gun discharges, and Alice is killed.

The majority of students selected (A). Identify their error, select the right answer and provide a concise rationale.

Comment: The word "immediately" raises a red flag for me. Remember that when you see a statute, the question will almost always turn on whether or not the statute was violated. "Immediately" is not consistent or synonymous with "premeditation" and "deliberation."

The problem with (A) is reconciling the word "immediately" in the answer choice with the requirement of "premeditation and deliberation" in the statute. The word "immediately" triggers heat of passion or voluntary manslaughter, not murder. Of the remaining choices, (B) most likely meets the terms of the statute. We are told that the defendant did two things: (1) He bought the poison and (2) he put the poison in the coffee. Logically, there was an interim time period between those two acts that allows for premeditation and deliberation.

B. Learning Through a *Wrong* Answer Example II

Alan, who was already married, went through a marriage ceremony with Betty and committed bigamy. Carl, his friend, who did not know of Alan's previous marriage, had encouraged Alan to marry Betty and was best man at the ceremony. If Carl is charged with being an accessory to bigamy, he should be found

(A) Not guilty, because his encouragement and assistance was not the legal cause of the crime.
(B) Not guilty, because he did not have the mental state required for aiding and abetting.
(C) Guilty, because he encouraged Alan, and his mistake as to the existence of a prior marriage is not a defense to the charge of bigamy.
(D) Guilty, because he was present when the crime occurred and thus is a principal in the second degree.

The majority of students selected (C). Identify their error, select the right answer and provide a concise rationale.

Comment: When I see a mistake in a criminal law question, I know I have to classify it as a "mistake of fact" or "mistake of law." The distinction is critical because I know that a mistake of fact may negate the intent element of a crime, but a mistake of law (criminal defendant did not know the criminal consequences of his act) is rarely an effective defense.

The error made was most likely caused by a misunderstanding or mis-application of the requirements for accomplice liability. (C) is wrong because mistake of fact (the existence of the prior marriage) is a defense to the charge of bigamy because it negates the intent element. In order to be found guilty as an accomplice for the underlying crime (here, bigamy), Carl has to have the requisite mental state. This would require Carl to have the mental state necessary to commit bigamy. Here, Carl didn't know of Alan's previous marriage, so he had no intent to commit bigamy and (B) is therefore the correct answer.

C. *Wrong* Answer Exercises

Constitutional Law

1. Leonard was the high priest of a small cult of Satan worshippers living in New Arcadia. As a part of the practice of their religious beliefs, a cat was required to be sacrificed to the glory of Satan after a live dissection of the animal in which it endured frightful pain. In the course of such religious sacrifice, Leonard was arrested on the complaint of the local Humane Society and charged under a statute punishing cruelty to animals. On appeal, a conviction of Leonard probably will be

Hint: Is the purpose of this statute to interfere with religion?

   (A) Sustained on the grounds that belief in or worship of Satan does not enjoy constitutional protection.
   (B) Sustained on the grounds that sincere religious belief is not an adequate defense on these facts.
   (C) Overturned on the grounds that the constitutionally guaranteed freedom of religion and its expression was violated.
   (D) Overturned on the grounds that the beliefs of the cult members in the need for the sacrifice might be reasonable, and their act was religious.

   The majority of students selected (C). Identify their error, select the right answer, and provide a concise rationale.

   _____

   _____

_____

_____

_____

_____

_____

_____

2. The legislature of State X enacts a statute that it believes reconciles the state's interest in the preservation of human life with a woman's right to reproductive choice. That statute permits a woman to have an abortion on demand during the first trimester of pregnancy but prohibits a woman from having an abortion after that time unless her physician determines that the abortion is necessary to protect the woman's life or health. If challenged on constitutional grounds in an appropriate court, this statute will probably be held

> **Reminder:** Whenever you see a statute challenged on constitutional grounds you should think about the level of scrutiny that applies and which party has the burden of proof—the challenger or the government.

   (A) constitutional, because the state has made a rational policy choice that creates an equitable balance between the compelling state interest in protecting fetal life and the fundamental right of a woman to reproductive choice.

   (B) constitutional, because recent rulings by the United States Supreme Court indicate that after the first trimester a fetus may be characterized as a person whose right to life is protected by the Due Process Clause of the Fourteenth Amendment.

   (C) unconstitutional, because the state has, without adequate justification, placed an undue burden on the fundamental right of a woman to reproductive choice prior to fetal viability.

   (D) unconstitutional, because a statute unqualifiedly permitting abortion at one stage of pregnancy and denying it at another, with only minor exceptions, establishes an arbitrary classification in violation of the Equal Protection Clause of the Fourteenth Amendment.

The majority of students selected (A). Identify their error, select the right answer, and provide a concise rationale.

_____

_____

_____

_____

_____

_____

_____

_____

3. A statute of the state of Texona prohibits any retailer of books, magazines, pictures, or posters from "publicly displaying or selling to any person any material that may be harmful to minors because of the violent or sexually explicit nature of its pictorial content." Violation of this statute is a misdemeanor. Corner Store publicly displays and sells magazines containing violent and sexually explicit pictures. The owner of this store is prosecuted under the above statute for these actions. In defending against this prosecution in a Texona trial court, the argument that would be the best defense for Corner Store is that the statute violates the

> *Hint:* Look how many times the word "any" is used in the first sentence: "any retailer," "any person," and "any material."

(A) First Amendment as it is incorporated into the Fourteenth Amendment, because the statute is excessively vague and overbroad.

(B) First Amendment as it is incorporated into the Fourteenth Amendment, because a state may not prohibit the sale of violent or sexually explicit material in the absence of proof that the material is utterly without any redeeming value in the marketplace of ideas.

(C) Equal Protection of the Laws Clause, because the statute irrationally treats violent and sexually explicit material that is pictorial differently from such material that is composed wholly of printed words.

(D) Equal Protection of the Laws Clause, because the statute irrationally distinguishes between violent and sexually explicit pictorial material that may harm minors and such material that may harm only adults.

The majority of students selected (B). Identify their error, select the right answer, and provide a concise rationale.

_____

_____

_____

_____

_____

_____

_____

_____

4. State Y has a state employee grievance system that requires any state employee who wishes to file a grievance against the state to submit that grievance for final resolution to a panel of 3 arbitrators chosen by the parties from a statewide board of 13 arbitrators. In any given case, the grievant and the state alternate in exercising the right of each party to eliminate five members of the board, leaving a panel of three members to decide their case. At the present time, the full board is composed of seven male arbitrators and six female arbitrators. Ellen, a female state employee, filed a sexual harassment grievance against her male supervisor and the state. Anne, the state's attorney, exercised all of her five strikes to eliminate five of the female arbitrators. At the time she did so, Anne stated that she struck the five female arbitrators solely because she believed women, as a group, would necessarily be biased in favor of another woman who was claiming sexual harassment. Counsel for Ellen eliminated four males and one female arbitrator, all solely on grounds of specific bias or conflicts of interest. As a result, the panel was all male.

When the panel ruled against Ellen on the merits of her case, she filed an action in an appropriate state court, challenging the panel selection process as a gender-based denial of Equal Protection of the Laws. In this case, the court should hold that the panel selection process is

(A) unconstitutional, because the gender classification used by the state's attorney in this case does not satisfy the requirements of intermediate scrutiny.

(B) unconstitutional, because the gender classification used by the state's attorney in this case denies the grievant the right to a jury made up of her peers.

(C) constitutional, because the gender classification used by the state's attorney in this case satisfies the requirements of the strict scrutiny test.

(D) constitutional, because the gender classification used by the state's attorney in this case satisfies the requirements of the rational basis test.

The majority of students selected (D). Identify their error, select the right answer, and provide a concise rationale.

5. An ordinance of Central City requires every operator of a taxicab in the city to have a license and permits revocation of that license only for "good cause." The Central City taxicab operator's licensing ordinance conditions the issuance of such a license on an agreement by the licensee that the licensee "not display in or on his or her vehicle any

bumper sticker or other placard or sign favoring a particular candidate for any elected municipal office." The ordinance also states that it imposes this condition in order to prevent the possible imputation to the city council of the views of its taxicab licensees and that any licensee who violates this condition shall have his or her license revoked. Driver, the holder of a Central City taxicab operator's license, decorates his cab with bumper stickers and other signs favoring specified candidates in a forthcoming election for municipal offices. A proceeding is initiated against him to revoke his taxicab operator's license on the sole basis of that admitted conduct. In this proceeding, does Driver have a meritorious defense based on the United States Constitution?

(A) No, because he accepted the license with knowledge of the condition and, therefore, has no standing to contest it.

(B) No, because a taxicab operator's license is a privilege and not a right and, therefore, is not protected by the Due Process Clause of the Fourteenth Amendment.

(C) Yes, because such a proceeding threatens Driver with a taking of property, his license, without just compensation.

(D) Yes, because the condition imposed on taxicab operators' licenses restricts political speech based wholly on its content, without any adequate governmental justification.

The majority of students selected (B). Identify their error, select the right answer, and provide a concise rationale.

6. As part of a comprehensive federal aid-to-education program, Congress included the following provisions as conditions for state receipt of federal funds: (1) Whenever textbooks are provided to students without charge, they must include no religious instruction and must be made available on the same terms to students in all public and private schools accredited by the state educational authority. (2) Salary supplements can be paid to teachers in public and private schools, up to 10% of existing salary schedules, where present compensation is less than the average salary for persons of comparable training and experience, provided that no such supplement is paid to any teacher who instructs in religious subjects. (3) Construction grants can be made toward the cost of physical plant at private colleges and universities, provided that no part of the grant is used for buildings in which instruction in religious subject matters is offered. Federal taxpayer Allen challenges the provision that allows the distribution of free textbooks to students in a private school where religious instruction is included in the curriculum. On the question of the adequacy of Allen's standing to raise the constitutional question, the most likely result is that standing will be

(A) sustained, because any congressional spending authorization can be challenged by any taxpayer.

(B) sustained, because the challenge to the exercise of congressional spending power is based on a claimed violation of specific constitutional limitations on the exercise of such power.

(C) denied, because there is insufficient nexus between the taxpayer and the challenged expenditures.

(D) denied, because in the case of private schools, no state action is involved.

The majority of students selected (C). Identify their error, select the right answer, and provide a concise rationale.

7. City enacted an ordinance banning from its public sidewalks all machines dispensing publications consisting wholly of commercial advertisements. The ordinance was enacted because of a concern about the adverse aesthetic effects of litter from publications distributed on the public sidewalks and streets. However, City continued to allow machines dispensing other types of publications on the public sidewalks. As a result of the City ordinance, 30 of the 300 sidewalk machines that were dispensing publications in City were removed. Is this City ordinance constitutional?

(A) Yes, because regulations of commercial speech are subject only to the requirement that they be rationally related to a legitimate state goal, and that requirement is satisfied here.

(B) Yes, because City has a compelling interest in protecting the aesthetics of its sidewalks and streets, and such a ban is necessary to vindicate this interest.

(C) No, because it does not constitute the least restrictive means with which to protect the aesthetics of City's sidewalks and streets.

(D) No, because there is not a reasonable fit between the legitimate interest of City in preserving the aesthetics of its sidewalks and streets and the means it chose to advance that interest.

The majority of students selected (C). Identify their error, select the right answer, and provide a concise rationale.

8. Congress enacts a criminal statute prohibiting "any person from interfering in any way with any right conferred on another person by the equal protection clause of the Fourteenth Amendment." Application of this statute to Jones, a private citizen, would be most clearly constitutional if Jones with threats of violence coerces

- (A) a public school teacher to exclude black pupils from her class, solely because of their race.
- (B) black pupils, solely because of their race, to refrain from attending a privately owned and operated school licensed by the state.
- (C) the bus driver operating a free school bus service under the sponsorship of a local church to refuse to allow black pupils on the bus, solely because of their race.
- (D) the federal office in charge of distributing certain federal benefits directly to students from distributing them to black pupils, solely because of their race.

The majority of students selected (D). Identify their error, select the right answer, and provide a concise rationale.

_____

_____

_____

_____

_____

_____

_____

9. Congress enacts a statute punishing "each and every conspiracy entered into by any two or more persons for the purpose of denying Black persons housing, employment, or education, solely because of their race." Under which of the following constitutional provisions is the authority of Congress to pass such a statute most clearly and easily justifiable?

   (A) The obligation of Contracts Clause.
   (B) The General Welfare Clause of Article I, §8.
   (C) The Thirteenth Amendment.
   (D) The Fourteenth Amendment.

   The majority of students selected (D). Identify their error, select the right answer, and provide a concise rationale.

   _____

   _____

   _____

   _____

   _____

   _____

   _____

   _____

10. Barnes was hired as an assistant professor of mathematics at Reardon State College and is now in his third consecutive one-year contract. Under state law he cannot acquire tenure until after five consecutive annual contracts. In his third year, Barnes was notified that he was not being rehired for the following year. Applicable state law and college rules did not require either a statement of reasons or a hearing, and in fact neither was offered to Barnes. Which of the following, if established, sets forth the strongest argument Barnes could make to compel the college to furnish him a statement of reasons for the failure to rehire him and an opportunity for a hearing?

(A) There is no evidence that tenured teachers are any more qualified than he is.
(B) He leased a home in reliance on an oral promise of re-employment by the college president.
(C) He was the only teacher at the college whose contract was not renewed that year.
(D) In the expectation of remaining at the college, he had just moved his elderly parents to the town in which the college is located.

The majority of students selected (C). Identify their error, select the right answer, and provide a concise rationale.

_____

_____

_____

_____

_____

_____

_____

11. John Doe, the owner of a milk container manufacturing firm, sought to focus public attention on the milk packaging law of the State of Clinton in order to have it repealed. On a weekday at 12:00 p.m., he delivered an excited, animated, and loud harangue on the steps of the State Capitol in front of the main entryway. An audience of 200 onlookers, who gathered on the steps, heckled him and laughed as he delivered his tirade. Doe repeatedly stated, gesturing expressively and making faces, that "the g-ddamned milk packaging law is stupid," and that "I will strangle every one of those g-ddamned legislators I can get hold of because this law they created proves they are all too dumb to live." After about 15 minutes, Doe stopped speaking, and the amused crowd dispersed. There are two relevant statutes of the State of Clinton. The first statute prohibits "all speech making, picketing, and public gatherings

of every sort on the Capitol steps in front of the main entryway between 7:45 a.m.-8:15 a.m., 11:45 a.m.-12:15 p.m., 12:45 p.m.-1:15 p.m., and 4:45 p.m.-5:15 p.m., on Capitol working days." A second state statute punishes "any person who shall intentionally threaten the life or safety of any public official for any act which he performed as part of his public office." Which of the following statements is correct concerning the possible punishment of Doe under the second statute?

(A) The statute is unconstitutional on its face.

(B) The statute is constitutional on its face, but Doe could not constitutionally be punished under it for this speech.

(C) Doe could constitutionally be punished under the statute for his speech.

(D) Doe could constitutionally be punished under the statute for his speech, but only if one or more legislators were actually present when he delivered it.

The majority of students selected (C). Identify their error, select the right answer, and provide a concise rationale.

_____

_____

_____

_____

_____

_____

_____

_____

12. Congress decides that the application of the Uniform Consumer Credit Code (UCCC) should be the same throughout the United States. To that end, it enacts the UCCC as a federal law directly applicable to all consumer credit, small loans, and retail installment sales. The law is intended to protect borrowers and buyers against unfair practices by suppliers of consumer credit. A national religious organization makes loans throughout the country for the construction and furnishing of churches. The federal UCCC would substantially interfere with the successful accomplishment of that organization's religious objectives. The organization seeks to obtain a declaratory judgment that the federal law may not be applied to its lending activities. As a matter of constitutional law, which of the following best describes the burden that must be sustained?

(A) The federal government must demonstrate that the application of this statute to the lending activities of this organization is necessary to vindicate a compelling governmental interest.

(B) The federal government must demonstrate that a rational legislature could believe that this law helps to achieve a legitimate national interest when applied to both religious and secular lending activities.

(C) The organization must demonstrate that no reasonable legislator could think that application of the UCCC to this organization would be helpful in accomplishing a legitimate governmental objective.

(D) The organization must demonstrate a specific congressional purpose to inhibit the accomplishment of the organization's religious objectives.

The majority of students selected (D). Identify their error, select the right answer, and provide a concise rationale.

_____

_____

_____

_____

_____

_____

_____

Contracts

13. Alpha and Beta made a written contract pursuant to which Alpha promised to convey a specified apartment house to Beta in return for Beta's promise (1) to convey a 100-acre farm to Alpha and (2) to pay Alpha $1,000 in cash six months after the exchange of the apartment house and the farm. The contract contained the following provision: "It is understood and agreed that Beta's obligation to pay $1,000 six months after the exchange of the apartment house and the farm shall be voided if Alpha has not, within three months after the aforesaid exchange, removed the existing shed in the parking area in the rear of the said apartment house." Which of the following statements concerning the order of performances is LEAST accurate?

(A) Alpha's tendering of good title to the apartment house is a condition precedent to Beta's duty to convey good title to the farm.

(B) Beta's tendering of good title to the farm is a condition precedent to Alpha's duty to convey good title to the apartment house.

(C) Beta's tendering of good title to the farm is a condition subsequent to Alpha's duty to convey good title to the apartment house.

(D) Alpha's tendering of good title to the apartment house and Beta's tendering of good title to the farm are concurrent conditions.

The majority of students selected (B). Identify their error, select the right answer, and provide a concise rationale.

_____

_____

_____

_____

_____

_____

14. Buyer mailed a signed order to Seller that read: "Please ship us 10,000 widgets at your current price." Seller received the order on January 7 and that same day mailed to Buyer a properly stamped, addressed, and signed letter stating that the order was accepted at Seller's current price of $10 per widget. On January 8, before receipt of Seller's letter, Buyer telephoned Seller and said, "I hereby revoke my order." Seller protested to no avail. Buyer received Seller's letter on January 9. Because of Buyer's January 8 telephone message, Seller never shipped the goods. Under the relevant and prevailing rules, is there a contract between Buyer and Seller as of January 10?

(A)   No, because the order was an offer that could be accepted only by shipping the goods; and the offer was effectively revoked before shipment.

(B)   No, because Buyer never effectively agreed to the $10 price term.

(C)   Yes, because the order was, for a reasonable time, an irrevocable offer.

(D)   Yes, because the order was an offer that Seller effectively accepted before Buyer attempted to revoke it.

The majority of students selected (A). Identify their error, select the right answer, and provide a concise rationale.

---

15. On May 1, Ohner telegraphed Byer, "Will sell you any or all of the lots in Grover subdivision at $5,000 each. Details follow in letter." The letter contained all the necessary details concerning terms of payment, insurance, mortgages, etc., and provided, "This offer remains open until June 1." On May 2, after he had received the telegram but before he had received the letter, Byer telegraphed Ohner, "Accept your offer with respect to lot 101." Both parties knew that there were 50 lots in the Grove subdivision and that they were numbered 101 through 150. Assume that on May 5, Ohner telephoned Byer that he had sold lots 102 through 150 to someone else on May 4 and that Byer thereafter telegraphed Ohner, "Will take the rest of the lots." Assume further that there is no controlling statute. In an action by Byer against Ohner for breach of contract, Byer probably will

(A) succeed, because Ohner had promised him that the offer would remain open until June 1.

(B) succeed, because Ohner's attempted revocation was by telephone.

(C) not succeed, because Byer's power of acceptance was terminated by Ohner's sale of the lots to another party.

(D) not succeed, because Byer's power of acceptance was terminated by an effective revocation.

The majority of students selected (C). Identify their error, select the right answer, and provide a concise rationale.

_____

_____

_____

_____

_____

_____

_____

16. In a single writing, Painter contracted with Farmer to paint three identical barns on her rural estate for $2,000 each. The contract provided for Farmer's payment of $6,000 upon Painter's completion of the work on

all three barns. Painter did not ask for any payment when the first barn was completely painted, but she demanded $4,000 after painting the second barn. Is Farmer obligated to make the $4,000 payment?

(A) No, because Farmer has no duty under the contract to pay anything to Painter until all three barns have been painted.

(B) No, because Painter waived her right, if any, to payment on a per-barn basis by failing to demand $2,000 upon completion of the first barn.

(C) Yes, because the contract is divisible.

(D) Yes, because Painter has substantially performed the entire contract.

The majority of students selected (C). Identify their error, select the right answer, and provide a concise rationale.

_____

_____

_____

_____

_____

_____

_____

17. Gourmet purchased the front portion of the land needed for a restaurant he desired to build and operate, but the back portion was the subject of a will dispute between Hope and Faith (two sisters). Hope's attorney advised her that her claim was doubtful. Gourmet, knowing only that the unresolved dispute existed, agreed in a signed writing to pay Hope $6,000, payable $1,000 annually, in exchange for a quitclaim deed (a deed containing no warranties) from Hope, who promptly executed such a deed to Gourmet and received Gourmet's first annual payment. Shortly thereafter, the probate court handed down a decision in Faith's favor, ruling that Hope had no interest in

the land. This decision has become final. Gourmet subsequently defaulted when his second annual installment came due. In an action against Gourmet for breach of contract, Hope will probably

(A) lose, because she was aware at the time of the agreement with Gourmet that her claim to the property quitclaimed was doubtful.

(B) lose, because Hope suffered no legal detriment in executing the quitclaim deed.

(C) win, because Gourmet bargained for and received in exchange a quitclaim deed from Hope.

(D) win, because Gourmet, by paying the first $1,000 installment, is estopped to deny that his agreement with Hope is an enforceable contract.

The majority of students selected (A). Identify their error, select the right answer, and provide a concise rationale.

_____

_____

_____

_____

_____

_____

_____

_____

18. During 1996 a series of arsons, one of which damaged the Humongous Store, occurred in the City of Swelter. In early 1997 Swelter's City Council adopted this resolution: "The City will pay $10,000 for the arrest and conviction of anyone guilty of any of the 1996 arsons committed here." The foregoing was telecast by the city's sole television station once daily for one week. Subsequently, Humongous, by a written memorandum to Gimlet, a private detective, proposed to pay Gimlet $200 "for each day's work you actually perform in investigating our fire." Thereafter, in August 1997, the City Council by resolution

repealed its reward offer and caused this resolution to be broadcast once daily for a week over two local radio stations, the local television station having meanwhile ceased operations. In September 1997, a Humongous employee voluntarily confessed to Gimlet to having committed all of the 1996 arsons. Humongous's president thereupon paid Gimlet at the proposed daily rate for his investigation and suggested that Gimlet also claim the city's reward, of which Gimlet had been previously unaware. Gimlet immediately made the claim. In December 1997, as a result of Gimlet's investigation, the Humongous employee was convicted of burning the store. The city, which has no immunity to suit, has since refused to pay Gimlet anything, although he swears that he never heard of the city's repeal before claiming its reward. In which of the following ways could the city's reward offer be effectively accepted?

(A) Only by an offeree's return promise to make a reasonable effort to bring about the arrest and conviction of an arsonist within the scope of the offer.
(B) Only by an offeree's making the arrest and assisting in the successful conviction of an arsonist within the scope of the offer.
(C) By an offeree's supplying information leading to arrest and conviction of an arsonist within the scope of the offer.
(D) By an offeree's communication of assent through the same medium (television) used by the city in making its offer.

The majority of students selected (B). Identify their error, select the right answer, and provide a concise rationale.

_____

_____

_____

_____

_____

_____

_____

_____

19. [Same fact pattern as previous question.] With respect to duration, the city's reward offer was terminable

(A) by lapse of time, on December 31 of the year in which it was made.
(B) not by lapse of time, but only by effective revocation.
(C) not by revocation, but only by lapse of a reasonable time.
(D) either by lapse of a reasonable time or earlier by effective revocation.

The majority of students selected (C). Identify their error, select the right answer, and provide a concise rationale.

_____

_____

_____

_____

_____

_____

_____

20. Fifty-year-old Ginrus wrote to Collatera, his unemployed adult niece and said: "If you come and live with me and take care of me and my property, Twin Oaks, for the rest of my life, I will leave Twin Oaks to you in my will." Collatera immediately moved in with Ginrus and took care of him and Twin Oaks until he was killed instantly in an automobile accident two weeks later. By his will, Ginrus left his entire estate, including Twin Oaks, to his unmarried sister, Sibling. Twin Oaks was reasonably worth $75,000. Assume that two days before Ginrus was killed, Collatera made an offer in writing to Drei to sell Twin Oaks to Drei for $75,000 when she should receive the property. If Drei has not accepted by the date of Ginrus's death, may Collatera effectively revoke her offer?

(A) Yes, because she could not make a valid offer to sell property she did not own.

(B) Yes, because there was no option contract with Drei.

(C) No, because a reasonable length of time had not elapsed since she made the offer.

(D) No, because the offer became irrevocable upon Ginrus's death.

The majority of students selected (A). Identify their error, select the right answer, and provide a concise rationale.

21. Kontractor agreed to build a power plant for a public utility. Subbo agreed with Kontractor to lay the foundation for $200,000. Subbo supplied goods and services worth $150,000, for which Kontractor made progress payments aggregating $100,000 as required by the subcontract. Subbo then breached by refusing unjustifiably to perform further. Kontractor reasonably spent $120,000 to have the work completed by another subcontractor. Subbo sues Kontractor for the reasonable value of benefits conferred, and Kontractor counterclaims for breach of contract. Which of the following should be the court's decision?

    (A) Subbo recovers $50,000, the benefit conferred on Kontractor for which Subbo has not been paid.

    (B) Subbo recovers $30,000, the benefit Subbo conferred on Kontractor minus the $20,000 in damages incurred by Kontractor.

    (C) Kontractor recovers $20,000, the excess over the contract price that was paid by Kontractor for the performance it had bargained to receive from Subbo.

(D) Neither party recovers anything, because Subbo committed a material, unexcused breach and Kontractor received a $50,000 benefit from Subbo for which Subbo has not been paid.

The majority of students selected (B). Identify their error, select the right answer, and provide a concise rationale.

_____

_____

_____

_____

_____

_____

_____

22. On November 1, the following notice was posted in a privately operated law school: "The faculty, seeking to encourage legal research, offers to any student at this school who wins the current National Obscenity Law Competition the additional prize of $500. All competing papers must be submitted to the Dean's office before May 1. (The National Competition is conducted by an outside agency, unconnected with any law school.)" Student read this notice on November 2, and thereupon intensified his effort to make his paper on obscenity law, which he started in October, a winner. Student also left on a counter in the Dean's office a signed note saying, "I accept the faculty's $500 Obscenity Competition offer." This note was inadvertently placed in Student's file and never reached the Dean or any faculty member personally. On the following April 1, the above notice was removed and the following substituted therefore: "The faculty regrets that our offer regarding the National Obscenity Law Competition must be withdrawn." Student's paper was submitted through the Dean's office on April 15. On May 1, it was announced that Student had won the National Obscenity Law Competition and the prize of $1,000.

The law faculty refused to pay anything. The promise of the faculty on November 1 was

(A) enforceable on principles of promissory estoppel.
(B) enforceable by Student's personal representative even if Student has been killed in an accident on April 16.
(C) not enforceable on policy grounds because it produced a non-commercial agreement between a student and his teachers, analogous to intramural family agreements and informal social commitments.
(D) not enforceable because Student, after entering the National Competition in October, was already under a duty to perform to the best of his ability.

The majority of students selected (A). Identify their error, select the right answer, and provide a concise rationale.

_____

_____

_____

_____

_____

_____

_____

_____

23. In September 1990, Joe Smith, 23 years old and unmarried, was beginning his third year of law school. At that time, he entered into a written lease with Landlord for the lease of an apartment for the nine-month school year ending on May 31, 1991, at $150 a month, payable in advance on the first day of each month. Joe paid the rent through December 1, but did not pay the amount due on January 1, nor has he paid any since. On January 15, 1991, Landlord threatened to evict Joe if he did not pay the rent. That night Joe called his father,

Henry, and told him that he did not have the money with which to pay the rent nor did he have the money with which to pay his tuition for the second semester. Henry told Joe that if he agreed not to marry until he finished law school, Henry would pay his tuition, the $150 rent that was due January 1, the rent for the rest of the school year, and $100 a month spending money until he graduated. Joe, who was engaged to be married at that time, agreed that he would not marry until after he graduated. On January 16, Henry wrote to Landlord the following letter which Landlord received on January 17: "Because of the love and affection which I bear my son, Joe, if you do not evict him, I will pay the rent he now owes you and will pay you his $150 rent on the first day of each month through May, 1991. If I do not hear from you by January 25, I will assume that this arrangement is all right with you. (Signed) Henry Smith." Landlord did not reply to Henry's letter and he did not evict Joe. Henry died suddenly on January 26. Joe continued to live in the apartment through May 31, 1991, but paid no more rent. He did not marry and graduated from law school. Henry had paid Joe's tuition for the spring semester, but had paid no money to either Landlord or Joe. Joe's claim against Henry's estate having been denied by the executor, Joe brought suit against the estate in June 1991, asking for a judgment of $400 ($100 spending money for each of the months, February through May). In this action, Joe probably will be

(A) successful.
(B) unsuccessful, because his contract with Henry was illegal.
(C) unsuccessful, because Henry's death terminated the offer.
(D) unsuccessful, because his contract with Henry was not in writing and signed by Henry.

The majority of students selected (C). Identify their error, select the right answer, and provide a concise rationale.

_____

_____

_____

24. While negligently driving his father's uninsured automobile, 25-year-old Arthur crashed into an automobile driven by Betty. Both Arthur and Betty were injured. Charles, Arthur's father, erroneously believing that he was liable because he owned the automobile, said to Betty: "I will see to it that you are reimbursed for any losses you incur as a result of the accident." Charles also called Physician and told him to take care of Betty, and that he, Charles, would pay the bill. Arthur, having no assets, died as a result of his injuries. Dodge, one of Arthur's creditors, wrote to Charles stating that Arthur owed him a clothing bill of $200 and that he was going to file a claim against Arthur's estate. Charles replied: "If you don't file a claim against Arthur's estate, I will pay what he owed you." Which of the following, if true, would be significant in determining whether or not there was bargained-for consideration to support Charles's promise to Physician?

  I.   Physician had not begun treating Betty before Charles called him.
  II. Charles had a contract with Betty.
      (A) I only.
      (B) II only.
      (C) Both I and II.
      (D) Neither I nor II.

The majority of students selected (A). Identify their error, select the right answer, and provide a concise rationale.

_____

_____

_____

_____

_____

_____

_____

25. [Same fact pattern as previous question.] If Physician discontinued treating Betty before she had fully recovered and Betty brought an action against Physician for breach of contract, which of the following arguments, if any, by Physician would probably be effective in defense?

    I.   Betty furnished no consideration, either express or implied.
   II. Physician's contract was with Charles and not with Betty.
 III. Whatever contract Physician may have had with Betty was discharged by novation on account of the agreement with Charles.

    (A) I only.
    (B) I and II only.
    (C) II and III only.
    (D) Neither I nor II nor III.

The majority of students selected (B). Identify their error, select the right answer, and provide a concise rationale.

_____

_____

_____

_____

_____

_____

_____

26. [Same fact pattern as question 24.] Assume that Charles, honestly believing that he owed Dodge nothing, refused to pay anything to Dodge, who honestly believed that Charles owed him $200. If Dodge then accepts $150 from Charles in settlement of the claim, will Dodge succeed in an action against Charles for the remaining $50?

(A) Yes, because Arthur's debt of $200 was liquidated and undisputed.
(B) Yes, because Dodge honestly believed that he had a legal right against Charles for the full $200.
(C) No, because Charles honestly believed that Dodge did not have a legal right against him for the $200.
(D) No, because Charles was not contractually obligated to pay Dodge $200 in the first place.

The majority of students selected (D). Identify their error, select the right answer, and provide a concise rationale.

_____

_____

_____

_____

_____

_____

_____

_____

27. In the application for a life insurance policy, Mary answered in the negative the question, "Have you ever had any heart disease?" Both the application and the insurance policy, which was issued, provided: "Applicant warrants the truthfulness of the statements made in the application and they are made conditions to the contract of insurance." Unknown to Mary, she had had a heart disease at a very early age. The policy provided that the proceeds were not to be paid over to the named beneficiary, Mary's daughter, Joan, "until she reaches the age of 21." No contingent beneficiary was named in the policy. Mary was killed in an automobile accident two months after the policy was issued. Joan died one month later at the age of 19 from injuries incurred in the same

accident. If the question is raised in an action against the insurance company, how is the court likely to construe the clause dealing with the truthfulness of statements in the application?

(A) The clause is a condition, and because the condition was not met, the company will not be liable.

(B) The clause is a condition, but it will be interpreted to mean, "truthfulness to the best of my knowledge."

(C) The clause is not a condition, and therefore the company may be liable even though Mary's statement was not true.

(D) The clause is not a condition but is a promise, and therefore the company will have a cause of action against Mary's estate for any losses it suffered because of Mary's misstatement.

The majority of students selected (A). Identify their error, select the right answer, and provide a concise rationale.

_____

_____

_____

_____

_____

_____

_____

_____

28. [Same fact pattern as previous question.] If no objection is made concerning Mary's misstatement in the application, how is the court most likely to construe the clause dealing with the payment of the proceeds to Joan?

(A) Joan's reaching the age of 21 is a constructive condition concurrent.

(B) Joan's reaching the age of 21 is a condition precedent to the insurance company's duty to pay anyone.

(C) Joan's reaching the age of 21 has legal significance only with respect to the time of payment.

(D) Joan's reaching the age of 21 has no legal significance.

The majority of students selected (B). Identify their error, select the right answer, and provide a concise rationale.

_____

_____

_____

_____

_____

_____

_____

_____

29. On June 1, Seller and Buyer contracted in writing for the sale and purchase of Seller's cattle ranch (a large single tract), and to close the transaction on December 1. On October 1, Buyer told Seller, "I'm increasingly unhappy about our June 1 contract because of the current cattle market, and do not intend to buy your ranch unless I'm legally obligated to do so." If Seller sues Buyer on October 15 for breach of contract, Seller will probably

(A) win, because Buyer committed a total breach by anticipatory repudiation on October 1.

(B) win, because Buyer's October 1 statement created reasonable grounds for Seller's insecurity with respect to Buyer's performance.

(C) lose, because the parties contracted for the sale and conveyance of a single tract, and Seller cannot bring suit for breach of such a contract prior to the agreed closing date.

(D) lose, because Buyer's October 1 statement to Seller was neither a repudiation nor a present breach of the June 1 contract.

The majority of students selected (A). Identify their error, select the right answer, and provide a concise rationale.

_____

_____

_____

_____

_____

_____

_____

30. Zeller contracted in writing to deliver to Baker 100 bushels of wheat on August 1 at $3.50 a bushel. Because his suppliers had not delivered enough wheat to him by that time, Zeller on August 1 only had 95 bushels of wheat with which to fulfill his contract with Baker. If Zeller tenders 95 bushels of wheat to Baker on August 1, and Baker refused to accept or pay for any of the wheat, which of the following best states the legal relationship between Zeller and Baker?

(A) Zeller has a cause of action against Baker, because Zeller has substantially performed his contract.

(B) Zeller is excused from performing his contract because of impossibility of performance.

(C) Baker has a cause of action against Zeller for Zeller's failure to deliver 100 bushels of wheat.

(D) Baker is obligated to give Zeller a reasonable time to attempt to obtain the other five bushels of wheat.

The majority of students selected (D). Identify their error, select the right answer, and provide a concise rationale.

_____

_____

---

31. On December 15, Lawyer received from Stationer, Inc., a retailer of office supplies, an offer consisting of its catalog and a signed letter stating, "We will supply you with as many of the items in the enclosed catalog as you order during the next calendar year. We assure you that this offer and the prices in the catalog will remain firm throughout the coming year." Assume that on January 15, having at that time received no reply from Lawyer, Stationer notified Lawyer that effective February 1, it was increasing the prices of certain specified items in its catalog. Is the price increase effective with respect to catalog orders Stationer receives from Lawyer during the month of February?

    (A)   No, because Stationer's original offer, including the price term, became irrevocable under the doctrine of promissory estoppel.

    (B)   No, because Stationer is a merchant with respect to office supplies and its original offer, including the price term, was irrevocable throughout the month of February.

    (C)   Yes, because Stationer received no consideration to support its assurance that it would not increase prices.

    (D)   Yes, because the period for which Stationer gave assurance that it would not raise prices was longer than three months.

The majority of students selected (C). Identify their error, select the right answer, and provide a concise rationale.

_____

_____

_____

_____

_____

_____

32. Bye Bye telegraphed Vendor on June 1, "At what price will you sell 100 of your QT-Model garbage disposal units for delivery around June 10?" Thereafter, the following communications were exchanged:

1. Telegram from Vendor received by Bye Bye on June 2: "You're in luck. We have only 100 QTs, all on clearance at 50% off usual wholesale of $120 per unit, for delivery at our shipping platform on June 12."
2. Letter from Bye Bye received in U.S. mail by Vendor on June 5: "I accept. Would prefer to pay in full 30 days after invoice."
3. Telegram from Vendor received by Bye Bye on June 6: "You must pick up at our platform and pay C.O.D."
4. Letter from Bye Bye received in U.S. mail by Vendor on June 9: "I don't deal with people who can't accommodate our simple requests."
5. Telegram from Bye Bye received by Vendor on June 10, after Vendor had sold and delivered all 100 of the QTs to another buyer earlier that day: "Okay. I'm over a barrel and will pick up the goods on your terms June 12."

Bye Bye now sues Vendor for breach of contract. Which of the following arguments will best serve Vendor's defense?

(A) Vendor's telegram received on June 2 was merely a price quotation, not an offer.
(B) Bye Bye's letter received on June 5 was not an acceptance because it varied the terms of Vendor's initial telegram.
(C) Bye Bye's use of the mails in response to Vendor's initial telegram was an ineffective method of acceptance.
(D) Bye Bye's letter received on June 9 was an unequivocal refusal to perform that excused Vendor even if the parties had previously formed a contract.

The majority of students selected (A). Identify their error, select the right answer, and provide a concise rationale.

_____

_____

_____

_____

_____

_____

_____

_____

Criminal Law

33. In which of the following situations is Defendant most likely to be guilty of common law murder?

    (A) During an argument in a bar, Norris punches Defendant. Defendant, mistakenly believing that Norris is about to stab him, shoots and kills Norris.

    (B) While committing a robbery of a liquor store, Defendant accidentally drops his revolver, which goes off. The bullet strikes and kills Johnson, a customer in the store.

    (C) While hunting deer, Defendant notices something moving in the bushes. Believing it to be a deer, Defendant fires into the bushes. The bullet strikes and kills Griggs, another hunter.

    (D) In celebration of the Fourth of July, Defendant discharges a pistol within the city limits in violation of a city ordinance. The bullet ricochets off the street and strikes and kills Abbott.

The majority of students selected (D). Identify their error, select the right answer, and provide a concise rationale.

_____

_____

_____

_____

_____

_____

_____

_____

34. In which of the following situations is Defendant most likely to be guilty of common law murder?

(A) Angered because his neighbor is having a noisy party, Defendant fires a rifle into the neighbor's house. The bullet strikes and kills a guest at the party.

(B) During an argument, Harry slaps Defendant. Angered, Defendant responds by shooting and killing Harry.

(C) Defendant drives his car through a red light and strikes and kills a pedestrian who is crossing the street.

(D) Using his fist, Defendant punches Walter in the face. As a result of the blow, Walter falls and hits his head on a concrete curb, suffers a concussion, and dies.

The majority of students selected (B). Identify their error, select the right answer, and provide a concise rationale.

_____

_____

_____

_____

_____

_____

35. In which of the following cases is a conviction of the named defendant for robbery LEAST likely to be upheld?

(A) Johnson forced his way into a woman's home, bound her, and compelled her to tell him that her jewelry was in an adjoining room. Johnson went into the room, took the jewelry, and fled.

(B) A confederate of Brown pushed a man in order to cause him to lose his balance and drop his briefcase. Brown picked up the brief-case and ran off with it.

(C) Having induced a woman to enter his hotel room, Ritter forced her to telephone her maid to tell the maid to bring certain jewelry to the hotel. Ritter locked the woman in the bathroom while he accepted the jewelry from the maid when she arrived.

(D) Hayes unbuttoned the vest of a man too drunk to notice and removed his wallet. A minute later, the victim missed his wallet and accused Hayes of taking it. Hayes pretended to be insulted, slapped the victim, and went off with the wallet.

The majority of students selected (C). Identify their error, select the right answer, and provide a concise rationale.

36. Harry met Bill, who was known to him to be a burglar, in a bar. Harry told Bill that he needed money. He promised to pay Bill $500 if Bill would go to Harry's house the following night and take some silverware. Harry explained to Bill that, although the silverware was legally his, his wife would object to his selling it. Harry pointed out his home, one of a group of similar tract houses. He drew a floor plan of the house that showed the location of the silverware. Harry said that his wife usually took several sleeping pills before retiring, and that he would make sure that she took them the next night. He promised to leave a window unlocked. Everything went according to the plan except that Bill, deceived by the similarity of the tract houses, went to the wrong house. He found a window unlocked, climbed in and found silver where Harry had indicated. He took the silver to the cocktail lounge where the payoff was to take place. At that point the police arrested the two men. If Harry were charged with burglary, his best argument for acquittal would be that

(A) there was no breaking.
(B) he consented to the entry.
(C) no overt act was committed by him.
(D) there was no intent to commit a felony.

The majority of students selected (B). Identify their error, select the right answer, and provide a concise rationale.

_____

_____

_____

_____

_____

_____

_____

37. [Same fact pattern as previous question.] Bill's best argument for acquittal of burglary is that he

(A) acted under a mistake of law.
(B) had the consent of the owner.
(C) reasonably thought he was in Harry's house.
(D) found the window unlocked.

The majority of at-risk students selected (B). Identify their error, select the right answer, and provide a concise rationale.

_____

_____

_____

_____

_____

_____

_____

_____

38. In which of the following situations is Defendant most likely to be guilty of the crime charged?

(A) Without the permission of Owner, Defendant takes Owner's car with the intention of driving it three miles to a grocery store and back. Defendant is charged with larceny.

(B) Defendant gets permission to borrow Owner's car for the evening by falsely promising to return it, although he does not intend to do so. Two days later, he changes his mind and returns the car. Defendant is charged with larceny by trick.

(C) Defendant gets permission to borrow Owner's car for the evening by misrepresenting his identity and falsely claiming he has a valid driver's license. He returns the car the next day. Defendant is charged with obtaining property by false pretenses.

(D) With permission, Defendant, promising to return it by 9:00 p.m., borrows Owner's car. Later in the evening, Defendant decides to keep the car until the next morning and does so. Defendant is charged with embezzlement.

The majority of students selected (A). Identify their error, select the right answer, and provide a concise rationale.

_____

_____

_____

_____

_____

_____

_____

_____

39. Joe and Marty were coworkers. Joe admired Marty's wristwatch and frequently said how much he wished he had one like it. Marty decided to give Joe the watch for his birthday the following week. On the weekend before Joe's birthday, Joe and Marty attended a company picnic. Marty took his watch off and left it on a blanket when he went off to join in a touch football game. Joe strolled by, saw the watch on the blanket, and decided to steal it. He bent over and picked up the watch. Before he could pocket it, however, Marty returned. When he saw Joe holding the watch, he said, "Joe, I know how much you like that watch. I was planning to give it to you for your birthday. Go ahead and take it now." Joe kept the watch. Joe has committed

(A) larceny.
(B) attempted larceny.
(C) embezzlement.
(D) no crime.

The majority of students selected (D). Identify their error, select the
right answer, and provide a concise rationale.

_____

_____

_____

_____

_____

_____

_____

40. At 11:00 p.m., John and Marsha were accosted in the entrance to their
apartment building by Dirk, who was armed as well as masked. Dirk
ordered the couple to take him into their apartment. After they entered
the apartment, Dirk forced Marsha to bind and gag her husband John
and then to open a safe that contained a diamond necklace. Dirk then
tied her up and fled with the necklace. He was apprehended by apartment building security guards. Before the guards could return to the
apartment, but after Dirk was arrested, John, straining to free himself,
suffered a massive heart attack and died. Dirk is guilty of

(A) burglary, robbery, and murder.
(B) robbery and murder only.
(C) burglary and robbery only.
(D) robbery only.

The majority of students selected (B). Identify their error, select the
right answer, and provide a concise rationale.

_____

_____

_____

_____

_____

_____

_____

_____

41. Tom had a heart ailment so serious that his doctors had concluded that only a heart transplant could save his life. They therefore arranged to have him flown to Big City to have the operation performed. Dan, Tom's nephew, who stood to inherit from him, poisoned him. The poison produced a reaction that required postponing the journey. The plane on which Tom was to have flown crashed, and all aboard were killed. By the following day, Tom's heart was so weakened by the effects of the poison that he suffered a heart attack and died. If charged with criminal homicide, Dan should be found

(A) guilty.

(B) not guilty, because his act did not hasten the deceased's death, but instead prolonged it by one day.

(C) not guilty, because the deceased was already suffering from a fatal illness.

(D) not guilty, because the poison was not the sole cause of death.

The majority of at-risk students selected (D). Identify their error, select the right answer, and provide a concise rationale.

_____

_____

_____

_____

_____

42. Johnson took a diamond ring to a pawnshop and borrowed $20 on it. It was agreed that the loan was to be repaid within 60 days and if it was not, the pawnshop owner, Defendant, could sell the ring. A week before expiration of the 60 days, Defendant had an opportunity to sell the ring to a customer for $125. He did so, thinking it unlikely that Johnson would repay the loan and, if he did, Defendant would be able to handle him somehow, even by paying him for the ring if necessary. Two days later, Johnson came in with the money to reclaim his ring. Defendant told him that it had been stolen when his shop was burglarized one night and that therefore he was not responsible for its loss. Larceny, embezzlement, and false pretenses are separate crimes in the jurisdiction. Suppose that, instead of denying liability, Defendant told Johnson the truth — that he sold the ring because he thought Johnson would not reclaim it — and offered to give Johnson $125. Johnson demanded his ring. Defendant said, "Look, buddy, that's what I got for it and it's more than it's worth." Johnson reluctantly took the money. Defendant could most appropriately be found guilty of

(A) Larceny.
(B) Embezzlement.
(C) False pretenses.
(D) None of the above.

The majority of students selected (D). Identify their error, select the right answer, and provide a concise rationale.

_____

_____

_____

43. John was fired from his job. Too proud to apply for unemployment benefits, he used his savings to feed his family. When one of his children became ill, he did not seek medical attention for the child at a state clinic because he did not want to accept what he regarded as charity. Eventually, weakened by malnutrition, the child died as a result of the illness. John has committed

(A) murder.
(B) involuntary manslaughter.
(C) voluntary manslaughter.
(D) no form of criminal homicide.

The majority of students selected (D). Identify their error, select the right answer, and provide a concise rationale.

_____

_____

_____

_____

_____

_____

_____

44. Jack and Paul planned to hold up a bank. They drove to the bank in Jack's car. Jack entered while Paul remained as lookout in the car. After a few moments, Paul panicked and drove off. Jack looked over the various tellers, approached one and whispered nervously, "Just hand over the cash. Don't look around, don't make a false move—or it's your life." The teller looked at the fidgeting Jack, laughed, flipped him a dollar bill and said, "Go on, beat it." Flustered, Jack grabbed the dollar and left. Soon after leaving the scene, Paul was stopped by the police for speeding. Noting his nervous condition, the police asked Paul if they might search the car. Paul agreed. The search turned up heroin concealed in the lid of the trunk. Paul's best defense to a charge of robbery would be that

(A) Jack alone entered the bank.
(B) Paul withdrew before commission of the crime when he fled the scene.
(C) Paul had no knowledge of what Jack whispered to the teller.
(D) The teller was not placed in fear by Jack.

The majority of students selected (B). Identify their error, select the right answer, and provide a concise rationale.

_____

_____

_____

_____

_____

_____

_____

Evidence

45. In a jurisdiction without a Dead Man's Statute, Parker's estate sued Davidson claiming that Davidson had borrowed from Parker $10,000, which had not been repaid as of Parker's death. Parker was run over by a truck. At the accident scene, while dying from massive injuries, Parker told Officer Smith to "make sure my estate collects the $10,000 I loaned to Davidson." Smith's testimony about Parker's statement is

(A) inadmissible, because it is more unfairly prejudicial than probative.
(B) inadmissible, because it is hearsay not within any exception.
(C) admissible as an excited utterance.
(D) admissible as a statement under belief of impending death.

The majority of students selected (D). Identify their error, select the right answer, and provide a concise rationale.

_____

_____

_____

_____

_____

_____

_____

46. Susan entered a guilty plea to a charge of embezzlement. Her attorney hired a retired probation officer as a consultant to gather information for the preparation of a sentencing plan for Susan that would avoid jail. For that purpose, the consultant interviewed Susan for three hours. Thereafter, the prosecution undertook an investigation of Susan's possible involvement in other acts of embezzlement. The consultant was subpoenaed to testify before a grand jury. The consultant refused to answer any questions concerning her conversation with Susan. The prosecution has moved for an order requiring her to answer those questions. The motion should be

(A) denied, on the basis of the attorney-client privilege.
(B) denied, in the absence of probable cause to believe the interview developed evidence relevant to the grand jury's inquiry.
(C) granted, because the consultant is not an attorney.
(D) granted, because exclusionary evidentiary rules do not apply in grand jury proceedings.

The majority of students selected (C). Identify their error, select the right answer, and provide a concise rationale.

_____

_____

_____

_____

_____

_____

_____

47. While crossing Spruce Street, Pesko was hit by a car that she did not see. Pesko sued Dorry for her injuries. At trial, Pesko calls Williams, a police officer, to testify that, ten minutes after the accident, a driver stopped him and said, "Officer, a few minutes ago I saw a hit-and run accident on Spruce Street involving a blue convertible, which I followed to the drive-in restaurant at Oak and Third," and that a few seconds later Williams saw Dorry sitting alone in a blue convertible in the drive-in restaurant's parking lot. Williams's testimony about the driver's statement should be

(A) admitted as a statement of recent perception.
(B) admitted as a present sense impression.
(C) excluded, because it is hearsay not within any exception.
(D) excluded, because it is more prejudicial than probative.

The majority of students selected (B). Identify their error, select the right answer, and provide a concise rationale.

_____

_____

_____

_____

_____

_____

_____

_____

48. Mary Webb, a physician, called as a witness by the defendant in the case *Parr v. Doan*, was asked to testify to statements made by Michael Zadok, her patient, for the purpose of obtaining treatment from Dr. Webb. Which of the following is the best basis for excluding evidence of Zadok's statements in a jurisdiction with a doctor-patient privilege?

(A) An objection by Dr. Webb asserting her privilege against disclosure of confidential communications made by a patient.

(B) An objection by Parr's attorney on the grounds of the doctor-patient privilege.

(C) A finding by the trial judge that Zadok had left the office without actually receiving treatment.

(D) The assertion of a privilege by Zadok's attorney, present at the trial as a spectator at Zadok's request, and allowed by the trial judge to speak.

The majority of students selected (A). Identify their error, select the right answer, and provide a concise rationale.

_____

_____

_____

_____

_____

---

49. Pedestrian died from injuries caused when Driver's car struck him.
Executor, Pedestrian's executor, sued Driver for wrongful death. At
trial, Executor calls Nurse to testify that two days after the accident, Pedestrian said to Nurse, "The car that hit me ran the red light."
Fifteen minutes thereafter, Pedestrian died. As a foundation for introducing evidence of Pedestrian's statement, Executor offers to the
court Doctor's affidavit that Doctor was the intern on duty the day
of Pedestrian's death and that several times that day Pedestrian had
said that he knew he was about to die. Is the affidavit properly considered by the court in ruling on the admissibility of Pedestrian's
statement?

(A) No, because it is hearsay not within any exception.
(B) No, because it is irrelevant since dying declarations cannot be used
except in prosecutions for homicide.
(C) Yes, because, though hearsay, it is a statement of then-existing
mental condition.
(D) Yes, because the judge may consider hearsay in ruling on
preliminary questions.

**The majority of students selected (C). Identify their error, select the
right answer, and provide a concise rationale.**

---

50. In an arson prosecution, the government seeks to rebut Defendant's alibi that he was in a jail in another state at the time of the fire. The government calls Witness to testify that he diligently searched through all the records of the jail and found no record of Defendant's having been incarcerated there during the time Defendant specified. The testimony of Witness is

   (A) admissible as evidence of absence of an entry from a public record.
   (B) admissible as a summary of voluminous documents.
   (C) inadmissible, because it is hearsay not within any exception.
   (D) inadmissible, because the records themselves must be produced.

   The majority of students selected (D). Identify their error, select the right answer, and provide a concise rationale.

   _____

   _____

   _____

   _____

   _____

   _____

   _____

   _____

51. Defendant is on trial for robbing a bank in State A. She testified that she was in State B at the time of the robbery. Defendant calls her friend, Witness, to testify that two days before the robbery Defendant told him that she was going to spend the next three days in State B. Witness's testimony is

(A) admissible, because the statement falls within the present sense impression exception to the hearsay rule.
(B) admissible, because a statement of plans falls within the hearsay exception for then-existing state of mind.
(C) inadmissible, because it is offered to establish an alibi by Defendant's own statement.
(D) inadmissible, because it is hearsay not within any exception.

The majority of students selected (D). Identify their error, select the right answer, and provide a concise rationale.

_____

_____

_____

_____

_____

_____

_____

_____

52. Defendant is on trial for participating in a drug sale. The prosecution calls Witness, an undercover officer, to testify that, when Seller sold the drugs to Witness, Seller introduced Defendant to Witness as "my partner in this" and Defendant shook hands with Witness but said nothing. Witness's testimony is

(A) inadmissible, because there is no evidence that Seller was authorized to speak for Defendant.
(B) inadmissible, because the statement of Seller is hearsay not within any exception.
(C) admissible as a statement against Defendant's penal interest.
(D) admissible as Defendant's adoption of Seller's statement.

The majority of students selected (B). Identify their error, select the
right answer, and provide a concise rationale.

_____

_____

_____

_____

_____

_____

_____

53. Miller is tried for armed robbery of the First Bank of City. The prosecution, in its case in chief, offers evidence that when Miller was arrested
one day after the crime, he had a quantity of heroin and a hypodermic
needle in his possession. At the request of police, the teller who was
robbed prepared a sketch bearing a strong likeness to Miller, but the
teller died in an automobile accident before Miller was arrested. At trial
the prosecution offers the sketch. The sketch is

(A) admissible as an identification of a person after perceiving him.
(B) admissible as past recollection recorded.
(C) inadmissible as hearsay not within any exception.
(D) inadmissible as an opinion of the teller.

The majority of students selected (B). Identify their error, select the
right answer, and provide a concise rationale.

_____

_____

_____

_____

54. Miller testified on direct examination that he had never been in the First Bank of City. His counsel asks, "What, if anything, did you tell the police when you were arrested?" If his answer would be, "I told them I had never been in the bank," this answer would be

    (A) admissible to prove Miller had never been in the bank.
    (B) admissible as a prior consistent statement.
    (C) inadmissible as hearsay not within any exception.
    (D) inadmissible, because it was a self-serving statement by a person with a substantial motive to fabricate.

    The majority of students selected (B). Identify their error, select the right answer, and provide a concise rationale.

Real Property

55. Testator devised his farm "to my son, Selden, for life, then to Selden's children and their heirs and assigns." Selden, a widower, had two

unmarried adult children. In appropriate action to construe the will, the court will determine that the remainder to children is

(A) indefeasibly vested.
(B) contingent.
(C) vested subject to partial defeasance.
(D) vested subject to complete defeasance.

The majority of students selected (A). Identify their error, select the right answer, and provide a concise rationale.

_____

_____

_____

_____

_____

_____

_____

_____

56. Anders conveyed her only parcel of land to Burton by a duly executed and delivered warranty deed, which provided: "To have and to hold the described tract of land in fee simple, subject to the understanding that within one year from the date of the instrument said grantee shall construct and thereafter maintain and operate on said premises a public health center." The grantee, Burton, constructed a public health center on the tract within the time specified and operated it for five years. At the end of this period, Burton converted the structure into a senior citizens' recreational facility. It is conceded by all parties in interest that a senior citizens' recreational facility is not a public health center. In an appropriate action, Anders seeks a declaration that the change in the use of the facility has caused the land and structure to revert to her. In this action, Anders should

(A) win, because the language of the deed created a determinable fee, which leaves a possibility of reverter in the grantor.

(B) win, because the language of the deed created a fee subject to a condition subsequent, which leaves a right of entry or power of termination in the grantor.

(C) lose, because the language of the deed created only a contractual obligation and did not provide for retention of property interest by the grantor.

(D) lose, because an equitable charge is enforceable only in equity.

The majority of students selected (B). Identify their error, select the right answer, and provide a concise rationale.

_____

_____

_____

_____

_____

_____

_____

_____

57. Otis owned in fee simple Lots 1 and 2 in an urban subdivision. The lots were vacant and unproductive. They were held as a speculation that their value would increase. Otis died and, by his duly probated will, devised the residue of his estate (of which Lots 1 and 2 were part) to Lena for life with remainder in fee simple to Rose. Otis's executor distributed the estate under appropriate court order and notified Lena that future real estate taxes on Lots 1 and 2 were Lena's responsibility to pay. Except for the statutes relating to probate and those relating to real estate taxes, there is no applicable statute. Lena failed to pay the real estate taxes due for Lots 1 and 2. To prevent a tax sale of the fee simple, Rose paid the taxes and demanded that Lena reimburse her for same. When Lena refused, Rose brought an appropriate action against Lena to recover the amount paid. In such action, Rose should recover

(A) the amount paid, because a life tenant has the duty to pay current charges.
(B) the present value of the interest that the amount paid would earn during Lena's lifetime.
(C) nothing, because Lena's sole possession gave the right to decide whether or not taxes should be paid.
(D) nothing, because Lena never received any income from the lots.

The majority of students selected (A). Identify their error, select the right answer, and provide a concise rationale.

_____

_____

_____

_____

_____

_____

_____

58. Olive owned Blackacre, a single-family residence. Fifteen years ago, Olive conveyed a life estate in Blackacre to Lois. Fourteen years ago, Lois, who had taken possession of Blackacre, leased Blackacre to Trent for a term of 15 years at the monthly rental of $500. Eleven years ago, Lois died intestate leaving Ron as her sole heir. Trent regularly paid rent to Lois and, after Lois's death, to Ron until last month. The period in which to acquire title by adverse possession in the jurisdiction is ten years. In an appropriate action, Trent, Olive, and Ron each asserted ownership of Blackacre. The court should hold that title in fee simple is in

(A) Olive, because Olive held a reversion and Lois has died.

(B) Ron, because Lois asserted a claim adverse to Olive when Lois executed a lease to Trent.

(C) Ron, because Trent's occupation was attributable to Ron, and Lois died 11 years ago.

(D) Trent, because of Trent's physical occupancy and because Trent's term ended with Lois's death.

The majority of students selected (A). Identify their error, select the right answer, and provide a concise rationale.

_____

_____

_____

_____

_____

_____

_____

_____

59. Theresa owned Blueacre, a tract of land, in fee simple. Theresa wrote and executed, with the required formalities, a will that devised Blueacre to "my daughter, Della, for life with remainder to my descendants *per stirpes*." At the time of writing the will, Theresa had a husband and no descendants living other than her two children, Della and Seth. Theresa died and the will was duly admitted to probate. Theresa's husband predeceased her. Theresa was survived by Della, Seth, four grandchildren, and one great grandchild. Della and Seth were Theresa's sole heirs at law. Della and Seth brought an appropriate action for declaratory judgment as to title of Blueacre. Guardians *ad litem* were appointed and all other steps were taken so that the judgment would bind all persons interested whether born or unborn. In that action, if the court rules that Della has a life estate in the whole of Blueacre and that the remainder is contingent, it will be

because the court chose one of several possible constructions and that the chosen construction

(A) related all vesting to the time of writing of the will.
(B) related all vesting to the death of Theresa.
(C) implied a condition that remaindermen survive Della.
(D) implied a gift of a life estate to Seth.

The majority of students selected (B). Identify their error, select the right answer, and provide a concise rationale.

_____

_____

_____

_____

_____

_____

_____

60. Orris had title to Brownacre in fee simple. Without Orris's knowledge, Hull entered Brownacre in 1950 and constructed an earthen dam across a watercourse. The earthen dam trapped water that Hull used to water a herd of cattle he owned. After 12 years of possession of Brownacre, Hull gave possession of Brownacre to Burns. At the same time, Hull also purported to transfer his cattle and all his interests in the dam and water to Burns by a document that was sufficient as a bill of sale to transfer personal property but was insufficient as a deed to transfer real property. One year later, Burns entered into a lease with Orris to lease Brownacre for a period of five years. After the end of the five-year term of the lease, Burns remained on Brownacre for an additional three years and then left Brownacre. At that time Orris conveyed Brownacre by a quitclaim deed to Powell. The period of time to acquire title by adverse possession in the jurisdiction is ten years. After Orris's conveyance to Powell, title to Brownacre was in

(A) Hull.
(B) Orris.
(C) Burns.
(D) Powell.

The majority of students selected (D). Identify their error, select the right answer, and provide a concise rationale.

_____

_____

_____

_____

_____

_____

_____

_____

Torts

61. An ordinance of City makes it unlawful to park a motor vehicle on a City street within ten feet of a fire hydrant. At 1:55 p.m. Parker, realizing he must be in Bank before it closed at 2:00 p.m. and finding no other space available, parked his automobile in front of a fire hydrant on a City street. Parker then hurried into the bank, leaving his aged neighbor, Ned, as a passenger in the rear seat of the car. About five minutes later, and while Parker was still in Bank, Driver was driving down the street. Driver swerved to avoid what he mistakenly thought was a hole in the street and sideswiped Parker's car. Parker's car was turned over on top of the hydrant, breaking the hydrant and causing a small flood of water. Parker's car was severely damaged and Ned was badly injured. There is no applicable guest statute. If City asserts a claim against Driver for the damage to the fire hydrant and Driver was negligent in swerving his car, his negligence is

(A) a cause in fact and a legal cause of City's harm.
(B) a cause in fact, but not a legal cause, of City's harm because Parker parked illegally.

    (C)   a legal cause, but not a cause in fact, of City's harm because Parker's car struck the hydrant.

    (D)   neither a legal cause nor a cause in fact of City's harm.

The majority of students selected (B). Identify their error, select the right answer, and provide a concise rationale.

_____

_____

_____

_____

_____

_____

_____

62. Si was in the act of siphoning gasoline from Neighbor's car in Neighbor's garage and without his consent when the gasoline exploded and a fire followed. Rescuer, seeing the fire, grabbed a fire extinguisher from his car and put out the fire, saving Si's life and Neighbor's car and garage. In doing so, Rescuer was badly burned. If Rescuer asserts a claim against Si for personal injuries, Rescuer will

    (A)   prevail, because he saved Si's life.

    (B)   prevail, because Si was at fault in causing the fire.

    (C)   not prevail, because Rescuer knowingly assumed the risk.

    (D)   not prevail, because Rescuer's action was not a foreseeable consequence of Si's conduct.

The majority of students selected (C). Identify their error, select the right answer, and provide a concise rationale.

_____

_____

_____

_____

_____

_____

_____

_____

63. Adam's car sustained moderate damage in a collision with a car driven by Basher. The accident was caused solely by Basher's negligence. Adam's car was still drivable after the accident. Examining the car the next morning, Adam could see that a rear fender had to be replaced. He also noticed that gasoline had dripped onto the garage floor. The collision had caused a small leak in the gasoline tank. Adam then took the car to Mechanic, who owns and operates a body shop, and arranged with Mechanic to repair the damage. During their discussion Adam neglected to mention the gasoline leakage. Thereafter, while Mechanic was loosening some of the damaged material with a hammer, he caused a spark, igniting vapor and gasoline that had leaked from the fuel tank. Mechanic was severely burned. Mechanic has brought an action to recover damages against Adam and Basher. The jurisdiction has adopted a pure comparative-negligence rule in place of the traditional common law rule of contributory negligence. In this action, will Mechanic obtain a judgment against Basher?

(A) No, unless there is evidence that Basher was aware of the gasoline leak.
(B) No, if Mechanic would not have been harmed had Adam warned him about the gasoline leak.
(C) Yes, unless Mechanic was negligent in not discovering the gasoline leak himself.
(D) Yes, if Mechanic's injury was a proximate consequence of Basher's negligent driving.

The majority of students selected (B). Identify their error, select the right answer, and provide a concise rationale.

_____

_____

_____

_____

_____

_____

_____

_____

64. While approaching an intersection with the red light against him, Motorist suffered a heart attack that rendered him unconscious. Motorist's car struck Child, who was crossing the street with the green light in her favor. Under the state motor vehicle code, it is an offense to drive through a red traffic light. Child sued Motorist to recover for her injuries. At trial it was stipulated that (1) immediately prior to suffering the heart attack, Motorist had been driving within the speed limit, had seen the red light, and had begun to slow his car; (2) Motorist had no history of heart disease and no warning of this attack; (3) while Motorist was unconscious, his car ran the red light. On cross motions for directed verdicts on the issue of liability at the conclusion of the proofs, the court should

(A) grant Child's motion, because Motorist ran a red light in violation of the motor vehicle code.

(B) grant Child's motion, because, in the circumstances, reasonable persons would infer that Motorist was negligent.

(C) grant Motorist's motion, because he had no history of heart disease or warning of the heart attack.

(D) deny both motions and submit the case to the jury, to determine whether, in the circumstances, Motorist's conduct was that of a reasonably prudent person.

The majority of students selected (D). Identify their error, select the right answer, and provide a concise rationale.

_____

_____

65. Motorco is a manufacturer of motor vehicles. A federal regulation requires that all motor vehicles manufactured for sale in the United States be equipped with seat belts for each passenger and prescribes specifications for such belts. Motorco equipped all its cars with seat belts. It purchased all the bolts used in its seat belt assemblies from Boltco, and it tested samples from each shipment received. Dunn purchased a motor vehicle manufactured by Motorco. While operating the car, with Price as a passenger in the front seat, Dunn collided with another vehicle. The collision was due solely to Dunn's negligence. Price had his seat belt fastened, but one of the bolts that anchored the belt to the frame broke. Price was thrown through the windshield, sustaining various injuries. Dunn, whose belt was fastened and held, was killed when, following the collision, the car went off the road, down an embankment, and overturned. Subsequent to the accident, tests of the bolt that broke showed metallurgical defects. Motorco's records showed that tests of samples from the shipment in which the defective bolt was received revealed no defective bolts. In a negligence action by Price against Motorco, the negligence of Dunn will be considered to be

(A) within the risk created by the action of Motorco.
(B) the proximate cause of Price's injuries.
(C) the legal cause of Price's injuries.
(D) an independent, intervening cause of Price's injuries.

The majority of students selected (B). Identify their error, select the right answer, and provide a concise rationale.

_____

_____

_____

_____

_____

_____

66. Dever drove his car into an intersection and collided with a fire engine that had entered the intersection from Dever's right. The accident was caused by negligence on Dever's part. As a result of the accident, the fire engine was delayed in reaching Peters' house, which was entirely consumed by fire. Peters' house was located about ten blocks from the scene of the accident. If Peters asserts a claim against Dever, Peters will recover

(A) the part of his loss that would have been prevented if the collision had not occurred.

(B) the value of his house before the fire.

(C) nothing, if Dever had nothing to do with causing the fire.

(D) nothing, because Dever's conduct did not create an apparent danger to Peters.

The majority of students selected (C). Identify their error, select the right answer, and provide a concise rationale.

_____

_____

_____

_____

_____

67. Roofer entered into a written contract with Orissa to repair the roof of Orissa's home, the repairs to be done "in a workmanlike manner." Roofer completed the repairs and took all of his equipment away, with the exception of a 20-foot extension ladder, which was left against the side of the house. He intended to come back and get the ladder the next morning. At that time, Orissa and her family were away on a trip. During the night, a thief, using the ladder to gain access to an upstairs window, entered the house and stole some valuable jewels. Orissa has asserted a claim against Roofer for damages for the loss of the jewels. In her claim against Roofer, Orissa will

(A) prevail, because by leaving the ladder Roofer became a trespasser on Orissa's property.
(B) prevail, because by leaving the ladder, Roofer created the risk that a person might unlawfully enter the house.
(C) not prevail, because the act of the thief was a superseding cause.
(D) not prevail, because Orissa's claim is limited to damages for breach of contract.

The majority of students selected (C). Identify their error, select the right answer, and provide a concise rationale.

68. Walker, a pedestrian, started north across the street in a clearly marked north-south crosswalk with the green traffic light in her favor. Walker was in a hurry, and so before reaching the north curb on the street, she cut to her left diagonally across the street to the east-west crosswalk and started across it. Just after reaching the east-west crosswalk, the traffic light turned green in her favor. She proceeded about five steps further across the street to the west in the crosswalk when she was struck by a car approaching from her right that she thought would stop but did not. The car was driven by Driver, 81 years of age, who failed to stop his car after seeing that the traffic light was red against him. Walker has a bone disease, resulting in very brittle bones, that is prevalent in only 0.02 percent of the population. As a result of the impact, Walker suffered a broken leg and the destruction of her family heirloom, a Picasso original painting that she was taking to her bank for safekeeping. The painting had been purchased by Walker's grandmother for $750 but was valued at $500,000 at the time of the accident. Walker has filed suit against Driver. Driver's attorney has alleged that Walker violated a state statute requiring that pedestrians stay in crosswalks, and that if Walker had not violated the statute she would have had to walk 25 feet more to reach the impact point and therefore would not have been at a place where she could have been hit by Driver. Walker's attorney ascertains that there is a statute as alleged by Driver, that his measurements are correct, that there is a state statute requiring observance of traffic lights, and that Driver's license expired two years prior to the collision. The violation of the crosswalk statute by Walker should not defeat her cause of action against Driver because

(A) Driver violated the traffic light statute at a later point in time than Walker's violation.
(B) Pedestrians are entitled to assume that automobile drivers will obey the law.
(C) Walker was hit while in the crosswalk.
(D) The risks that the statute was designed to protect against probably did not include an earlier arrival at another point.

The majority of students selected (C). Identify their error, select the right answer, and provide a concise rationale.

_____

_____

_____

_____

_____

_____

_____

69. Pat had been under the care of a cardiologist for three years prior to submitting to an elective operation that was performed by Surgeon. Two days thereafter, Pat suffered a stroke, resulting in a coma, caused by a blood clot that lodged in her brain. When it appeared that she had entered a permanent vegetative state, with no hope of recovery, the artificial life support system that had been provided was withdrawn, and Pat died a few hours later. The withdrawal of artificial life support had been requested by her family and was duly approved by a court. Surgeon was not involved in that decision, or in its execution. The administrator of Pat's estate thereafter filed a wrongful death action against Surgeon, claiming that Surgeon was negligent in having failed to consult a cardiologist prior to the operation. At the trial the plaintiff offered evidence that accepted medical practice would require examination of Pat by a cardiologist prior to the type of operation that Surgeon performed. In this action, the plaintiff should

(A) prevail, if Surgeon was negligent in failing to have Pat examined by a cardiologist prior to the operation.
(B) prevail, if the blood clot that caused Pat's death was caused by the operation which Surgeon performed.
(C) not prevail, absent evidence that a cardiologist, had one examined Pat before the operation, would probably have provided advice that would have changed the outcome.
(D) not prevail, because Surgeon had nothing to do with the withdrawal of artificial life support, which was the cause of Pat's death.

The majority of students selected (B). Identify their error, select the right answer, and provide a concise rationale.

_____

_____

_____

_____

_____

_____

_____

_____

70. Traveler was a passenger on a commercial aircraft owned and operated by Airline. The aircraft crashed into a mountain, killing everyone on board. The flying weather was good. Traveler's legal representative brought a wrongful death action against Airline. At trial, the legal representative offered no expert or other testimony as to the cause of the crash. On Airline's motion to dismiss at the conclusion of the legal representative's case, the court should

   (A) grant the motion, because the legal representative has offered no evidence as to the cause of the crash.
   (B) grant the motion, because the legal representative has failed to offer evidence negating the possibility that the crash may have been caused by mechanical failure that Airline could not have prevented.
   (C) deny the motion, because the jury may infer that the aircraft crashed due to Airline's negligence.
   (D) deny the motion, because in the circumstances common carriers are strictly liable.

The majority of students selected (A). Identify their error, select the right answer, and provide a concise rationale.

_____

_____

_____

_____

_____

_____

_____

_____

71. Passenger departed on an ocean liner knowing that it would be a rough voyage due to predicted storms. The ocean liner was not equipped with the type of lifeboats required by the applicable statute. Passenger was swept overboard and drowned in a storm so heavy that even a lifeboat that conformed to the statute could not have been launched. In an action against the operator of the ocean liner brought by Passenger's representative, will Passenger's representative prevail?

(A) Yes, because the ocean liner was not equipped with the statutorily required lifeboats.

(B) Yes, because in these circumstances common carriers are strictly liable.

(C) No, because the storm was so severe that it would have been impossible to launch a statutorily required lifeboat.

(D) No, because Passenger assumed the risk by boarding the ocean liner knowing that it would be a rough voyage.

The majority of students selected (A). Identify their error, select the right answer, and provide a concise rationale.

_____

_____

_____

_____

_____

_____

_____

72. Driver was driving his car near Owner's house when Owner's child darted into the street in front of Driver's car. As driver swerved and braked his car in order to avoid hitting the child, the car skidded up Owner's driveway and stopped just short of owner, who was standing in the driveway and had witnessed the entire incident. Owner suffered serious emotional distress from witnessing the danger to his child and to himself. Neither Owner nor his property was physically harmed. If Owner asserts a claim for damages against Driver, will Owner prevail?

(A) Yes, because Driver's entry onto Owner's land was unauthorized.
(B) Yes, because Owner suffered serious emotional distress by witnessing the danger to his child and himself.
(C) No, unless Driver was negligent.
(D) No, unless Owner's child was exercising reasonable care.

The majority of students selected (B). Identify their error, select the right answer, and provide a concise rationale.

_____

_____

_____

_____

_____

_____

_____

_____

73. Del's sporting goods shop was burglarized by an escaped inmate from a nearby prison. The inmate stole a rifle and bullets from a locked cabinet. The burglar alarm at Del's shop did not go off because Del had negligently forgotten to activate the alarm's motion detector. Shortly thereafter, the inmate used the rifle and ammunition stolen from Del in a shooting spree that caused injury to several people, including Paula. If Paula sues Del for the injury she suffered, will Paula prevail?

(A) Yes, if Paula's injury would have been prevented had the motion detector been activated.

(B) Yes, because Del was negligent in failing to activate the motion detector.

(C) No, because the storage and sale of firearms and ammunition is not an abnormally dangerous activity.

(D) No, unless there is evidence of circumstances suggesting a high risk of theft and criminal use of firearms stocked by Del.

The majority of students selected (A). Identify their error, select the right answer, and provide a concise rationale.

_____

_____

_____

_____

_____

_____

_____

_____

D. Correct Answers for *Wrong* Answer Exercises

Constitutional Law

1. It is very important that you understand how to apply the Free Exercise Clause on the bar exam because it is relatively easy and the odds are you will see a related question. Here's what you need to know. If the statute is intentionally designed to interfere with religion it will usually be struck down as unconstitutional because it will not survive strict scrutiny: The government will be unable to prove the law interfering with religious

practice is necessary to achieve a compelling state interest. If, on the other hand, the law incidentally interferes with religious practice, but religion is not specifically targeted, the law may be constitutional. For the bar exam, you should look for a generally applicable criminal law or regulation. Here, the statute that criminalizes cruelty to animals applies to everyone. The statute was not enacted for the purpose of preventing this religious group from practicing the tenets of their religion. Because it is a generally applicable criminal law, the correct answer is (B), not (C).

2. You should not miss any question that applies to the type of scrutiny or test a court will apply to constitutionally related questions. The levels of scrutiny and other constitutional tests are a matter of memorization and mechanical application. Here we have an abortion statute, and the reason why students incorrectly chose (A) are the kernels of true statements students recognize. A woman has a fundamental right to an abortion before viability and the state has a compelling interest in preserving life postviability. But there is no balancing test, as (A) suggests. This question is all about knowing the rule for analyzing abortion statutes: Previability, the government may not unduly burden a woman's fundamental right to an abortion. An undue burden is one that places a substantial obstacle in the way of a woman seeking an abortion. Postviability, the government may ban abortions as long as there is an exception to protect the health or life of the mother. (C) is the only option that correctly identifies the applicable test.

3. (B) states the right result for the wrong reason. You will earn many points on constitutional law questions simply by knowing and applying the correct test or level of scrutiny articulated by the Supreme Court. (B) looks logical and reasonable, and if you don't know the law, you might reasonably assume this should be the appropriate standard. The correct standard is that the work may be prohibited if, taken as a whole, it lacks serious literary, artistic, political, or scientific value. If (B) is the right result for the wrong reason, then (A) must be the correct choice. How would a retailer determine whether or not a picture is harmful to a minor? How does one determine whether the threshold for explicitness has been crossed? Because the terms of the statute are at best ambiguous, a retailer would not be able to reasonably ascertain what may or may not be displayed.

4. The purpose of this question is to reinforce the point made in the previous one: You *must* know the levels of constitutional scrutiny, which party has the corresponding burden of proof, and how to apply the correct test on fact patterns. The mistake students made in choosing (D) was simply not knowing the correct level of scrutiny for gender-based discrimination claims. Rational basis is not the correct test. Gender-based discrimination claims are subject to intermediate

scrutiny: The government has the burden of proving the law is substantially related to an important government interest. The correct answer is therefore (A).

5. Students who chose (B) thought the question turned on the process due when the government denies a privilege and concluded that procedural due process only applies when the government denies a right—specifically, life, liberty, or property. This question is fundamentally about a content-based restriction of speech. It is content-based because the restriction is on campaign bumper stickers, which is political speech. Content-based speech that is not otherwise considered "unprotected" is subject to strict scrutiny, which for the bar exam almost always means the government loses. The correct answer is (D) because the government will not be able to prove the ordinance is necessary in order to achieve a compelling government interest. The trap that students fall into on this question is focusing on the right/privilege distinction. Here, whether a license is a right or a privilege is irrelevant. The government can't distribute benefits (however characterized) based on one's willingness to forfeit constitutional rights (in this case, freedom of speech).

6. This question is an excellent example of the level of nuance often tested on the MBE. As a general proposition, most students remember that paying taxes is not enough for Article III standing to challenge a spending authorization, leading them to conclude that the correct answer is (C), which is wrong because of a limited exception. A taxpayer may sue if congress exercises power under the Taxing and Spending Clause and the enactment exceeds specific constitutional limitations. In other words, if the spending under that clause is allegedly for an unconstitutional purpose, a taxpayer has standing to sue. The unconstitutional purpose that may be discerned here is that the distribution of textbooks violates the First Amendment Establishment Clause. The critical lesson to take from this question is that you must know exceptions and limitations to rules as well as you know the rules themselves. The correct answer is (B).

7. The key to answering this question correctly lies in identifying the type of speech that is restricted and then applying the correct level of constitutional scrutiny. The banning of machines dispensing commercial advertisements is a restriction on commercial speech. The majority of students answering incorrectly selected (C), which is wrong because strict scrutiny doesn't apply to commercial speech. The least restrictive means test is inapplicable. The mistake students make is assuming commercial advertisements receive the same level of scrutiny as other content-based speech. Once the speech restriction is identified as commercially based, choice (D) is the only possible correct answer because it is the only one that articulates the test for mid-level scrutiny, which applies to commercial speech. An important

lesson to draw from this question is *if you see numbers in a question, presume they are very important*. Here, we are told the concern is for litter, yet only 10 percent of the machines were removed. There's a key piece missing from this fact pattern, and that is the link between commercial publications and litter. There is no study that shows that while they comprise only 10 percent of the dispensers that they contribute to a disproportionately high percentage of the litter problem. And 10 percent is not a lot, so the key here is to examine how the restriction furthers the goal and, in the absence of a disproportionate contribution to the problem, it doesn't.

8. It is critically important that you understand why (D) is wrong. The premise of this question revolves around a violation of the Fourteenth Amendment. (D) *must* be wrong because **the Equal Protection Clause of the Fourteenth Amendment does not apply to the federal government**. The Equal Protection Clause applies to state action. The Fifth Amendment's Due Process Clause has been interpreted to have an Equal Protection component that applies to the federal government, but **an answer that suggests the federal government is violating the Equal Protection Clause of the Fourteenth Amendment is *always* a wrong answer**. The requirement of state action also means that individuals cannot violate the Fourteenth Amendment unless they are state actors. (A) is the correct answer because a public school is a state actor. The teacher's act in excluding black pupils is a violation of the Equal Protection Clause and Jones is interfering with the rights of the black students by threatening the teacher with violence.

9. Every year, 75 percent of my students will choose (D). (D) is wrong because as discussed above, the Fourteenth Amendment only applies to state action. In the previous question, the school was a state actor and the Fourteenth Amendment was therefore applicable. Here, we are dealing with private citizens and the Fourteenth Amendment doesn't apply. Here's the takeaway point and what you need to know for the bar exam: The Thirteenth Amendment is the only constitutional amendment that applies to the conduct of private citizens. The correct answer is therefore (C).

10. This looks like a constitutional law question, but if you read carefully, you'll see why that's not the case. (C) implies the decision not to renew Barnes's contract was discriminatory because his was the only one not renewed. There are several problems with this choice. In order to find discrimination, one has to assume certain facts. Never assume facts on the bar exam! We are given no basis for discrimination (e.g., we don't know what race or religion Barnes is) nor are we told how many other teachers were eligible for contract renewal. The fact that he was the only one not renewed doesn't tell us how many others were similarly not renewed in the past. Barnes's strongest argument is based in equity.

He has no contract nor does there appear to be a constitutional argument. Barnes's best argument is that he relied on the oral promise of the president, choice (B), to his detriment (he leased a home and therefore suffered financially). The president's promise may be enforced under principles of promissory estoppel.

11. In order for (C) to be correct, the statute must be both constitutional on its face and constitutional as applied. Students who incorrectly selected this choice correctly identified the constitutionality of the statute. There is no constitutional problem with the law forbidding the threatening of a public official for acts performed as part of public office. The problem here is the applicability of the statute to Doe. The critical fact that you should have picked up on is the laughter and amusement of the crowd. The reason the statute is inapplicable to Doe and why (B) is the correct answer lies with the "clear and present danger" test. It cannot be said that Doe's rant was likely to incite imminent lawlessness. Why? Because the audience laughed; they didn't take Doe seriously. The takeaway point of this question is that every word matters in a fact pattern on the bar exam.

12. This is yet another question that highlights the importance of knowing the levels of scrutiny and tests for constitutional law questions. The mistake made by students choosing (D) is not knowing the correct test and burden. This question is about interfering with the free exercise of religion, a fundamental right. The law will therefore be subject to strict scrutiny, which *always* means the burden is on the government to prove the law is necessary to achieve a compelling state interest, and (A) is the correct answer. (D) is not only wrong, it is wrong for two reasons, which you should now be able to identify. The test stated in the answer choice is wrong *and* it places the burden of proof on the wrong party.

Contracts

13. Many students miss this question because of careless reading. The question asks for the *least* accurate description, not the *most* accurate. What does that mean for our thinking framework? There are three good answers, or answers that reasonably provide a fair reading of the facts. We are looking for the one bad or inaccurate description. The problem with (B) is that it is not inaccurate. In fact (B) and (A) are wrong for a reason that is unrelated to the substantive law of the question because they are really the same answer and there can only be one right answer for each question on the bar exam. Exchanging title to the farm could reasonably be seen as a condition precedent to exchanging title to the apartment; likewise, exchanging title to the apartment can be seen as a condition precedent to turning title over to the

farm. (C) is right because it is wrong! (C) does not accurately describe what is going on in the fact pattern. A condition subsequent is one that discharges a duty to perform. There is no such event in the facts. Each performance is a condition precedent to the other party's duty to perform. Tendering title does not discharge either party's duty to perform.

14. Contract formation is one of those categories that falls into the area of a "must win" in your bar preparation efforts. It is highly tested and well worth your time to learn all of the rules and nuances associated with offer and acceptance, particularly the "mailbox rule." The mistake in choosing (A) is not having adequate understanding of a relatively easy concept in contract formation. This is a question you cannot afford to miss. The rule you need to know is that an offer for the sale of goods may be accepted by shipment of the goods (as (A) suggests) *or* by a promise to ship the goods. Here, the offer was made and accepted on January 7. The acceptance became valid upon dispatch; therefore, the offer could not be revoked the next day, as (D) correctly states.

15. This is a contract for the sale of real estate, so the common law applies. If you apply the UCC, you will get this question wrong because you will choose (A). Option contracts require consideration at common law, but under the UCC, options only require good faith. (A) is wrong because there is no consideration for the option and we are subject to common law. (C) is a tempting answer because it arrives at the right result, but for the wrong reason. The sale of lots to someone else alone doesn't terminate Buyer's power of acceptance. As the correct answer (D) recognizes, it is Buyer's *knowledge* of the sale that terminates the power of acceptance. The knowledge of the sale to another party acts as an effective revocation. Remember, we are under the common law. Even if Seller promised to keep the offer open, Seller may revoke if Buyer doesn't pay consideration for the option.

16. This question highlights a very common error I see students make. This fact pattern contains nice round numbers. There are three barns and Farmer agrees to pay $2,000 to paint each. The total value of the contract is therefore $6,000. Painter paints two barns, the value of which is $4,000. We are told the value of painting each barn is the same, which makes (C) the tempting choice. The point, however, is that just because a contract is easily *divided* doesn't make that contract *divisible*. This question also reinforces the theme that reading carefully is paramount to success. We are told in the fact pattern that payment of $6,000 was to be made upon the painting of *all three* barns. Partial performance isn't enough. Once the Painter fully performed, Farmer had a duty to perform by paying the full amount, choice (A).

17. You can be sure that you will see more than one question testing your knowledge of consideration. Why do you think you were told that Hope's claim was "doubtful"? This question turns on the doubtful

nature of her claim. If Hope knew for sure that her claim was not valid, her promise would not be supported by consideration because she would not incur a legal detriment. However, even though the claim was in fact determined to be invalid, her surrender is considered to be supported by consideration because the claim was doubtful (not invalid) at the time of the bargain. The correct answer is therefore (C).

18. This question is testing your knowledge of reward offers. The early 1997 communication from City Council is clearly an offer, but is this an offer for a bilateral or unilateral contract? The distinction is critical in determining what constitutes a valid acceptance. A reward offer is an offer for a unilateral contract; it may only be accepted by complete performance. The City Council is not looking for a return promise to perform. The next step is determining what constitutes full performance, which is simply a matter of looking at the terms of the offer. The offer requires an arrest and conviction, as choice (C) correctly indicates. The problem with (B) is a misunderstanding or incorrect interpretation of "arrest and conviction." A reasonable interpretation would allow one to conclude that information leading to the arrest and conviction of the arsonist is full performance, while on the other hand, it would be unreasonable from an objective standpoint to believe that the City Council literally would require a member of the public to arrest and then assist the district attorney in convicting the arsonist.

19. Lapse of time and an effective revocation are two ways that will serve to terminate an offer, which is in fact the correct answer (D) here. So what mistake in reasoning did students make that led them to choose (C)? They incorrectly assumed reward offers are irrevocable, which is not the case.

20. This question is yet another example of the importance of careful reading. In essence, all we are being asked to do is recognize the ways offers may be revoked. The problem with (A) is that it doesn't state a reason for revocation of the offer. If Collatera offered to sell property she didn't own, that may be fraud but not a *reason* for an effective revocation. (A) illogically suggests that one may effectively revoke an ineffective offer. If the offer is ineffective *ab initio*, there is nothing to effectively revoke. The correct answer (B) is a straightforward statement of the common law rule: Offers that are not supported by consideration may be revoked prior to acceptance (even if assurances are made to the contrary).

21. The key concept for contract damages, a subject with which many law students experience difficulty, is knowing that the general rule or default measure is expectation damages. That is, the goal is to put the non-breaching party in the position she would have been in had the contract been performed. We are not looking to punish anyone financially for wrongful breach. Not to worry; this is not high-level math. We simply

need to figure out the total value of the contract to figure out damages. Here, the contract value was $200,000: Kontractor was to pay $200,000 to Subbo for a foundation. Kontractor paid $100,000 to Subbo per the agreement before Subbo breached. Kontractor had to pay another subcontractor $120,000 to finish the foundation. So Kontractor paid a total of $220,000. How much would Kontractor have paid if the contract had been performed? We are told in the fact pattern that Kontractor was to pay $200,000. It will take $20,000 to put Kontractor in the position it would have been in if Subbo performed, and (C) is the correct answer. (B) is wrong because Subbo isn't entitled to any recovery and because this answer choice doesn't put Kontractor in the position it would have been in had the contract been fully performed.

22. This question highlights one of the most common error students make. (A) *must* be a wrong answer because there is a valid contract. The doctrine of promissory estoppel does not apply to valid contracts; rather, it is an equitable remedy that acts as a substitute for consideration when the promisee detrimentally relies on a promise and that reliance is foreseeable. **The answer that a valid contract is enforceable at law under promissory estoppel is always a wrong answer** and something you should be on the lookout for. The correct answer is (B) because it recognizes the existence of a valid, enforceable contract. Once the student performed (or in this case continued to perform) with knowledge of the offer, the offer could not be revoked until the student had a reasonable amount of time to complete performance.

23. First observation: Do not give up on a question or think it will be difficult because it is relatively long. If you are pressed for time, that might be the correct strategy, but don't assume length correlates with difficulty. This is not a difficult question, but many students will give up a point here unnecessarily. Second observation: *True statements are not necessarily right answers*. (C) is a tempting answer because it contains a true statement: Death does terminate an offer. The reason (C) is wrong, however, is that Henry's offer had been accepted by Joe before Henry died. Death terminates an offer, but not a contract. The correct answer is (A), because the contract is enforceable.

24. This is another great example of why it is so important to read carefully. Our task is to determine if either or both of the statements helps in determining whether or not there was consideration to support the promise Charles made to the physician, not whether there was or wasn't valid consideration. So we are looking for evidence of a legal detriment. Let's look at the first statement: "Physician had not yet begun treating Betty before Charles called him." This should trigger the pre-existing legal duty doctrine. The fact that Physician hasn't started treatment necessarily means there is no pre-existing legal duty to treat Betty. Payment for treatment is the bargained-for consideration.

Had treatment begun, the promise to pay would not have induced the detriment (the treatment). So this first statement, if true, is very helpful to determine whether or not there was a bargained-for exchange of promises. The mistake students make, and the reason (A) is the wrong answer and (C) is correct, is not understanding the implication of the second statement — that Charles had a contract with Betty. The question is why a contract Charles has with Betty would be relevant to whether there is consideration for Charles's contract with physician. Most students will stop here, seeing no obvious connection. How can one set of promises bear on whether there is consideration for another set? If Charles had a contract to pay Betty for her medical expenses and Charles then makes a contract to pay the Physician for Betty's medical expenses, what happens to the contract with Betty? That contract would be discharged, a benefit to Charles that would be useful in determining whether there was a bargained-for exchange with the Physician. Charles has to pay for medical expenses, but he doesn't have to pay twice. Betty is the beneficiary of the contract between Charles and Physician because either way, her medical expenses are covered.

25. We are given three separate statements and are being asked which, if any, would be a good argument for the Physician in defense of a breach of contract case brought by Betty. Students will invariably lock on to the first statement, reasoning that no consideration means no contract and if there is no contract, Physician cannot be in breach. The problem is that Betty is the intended beneficiary of the valid contract (i.e., there was consideration for the contract) between Charles and Physician. Intended beneficiaries can enforce a valid contract, so the fact that Betty provided no consideration doesn't matter. Consideration was provided (by Charles), Betty was to get the benefit of the bargain (medical treatment), and Betty can enforce the contract. The same rationale applies to the second statement. The fact that the contract was between Charles and Physician doesn't mean Betty is without enforceable contractual rights. As the intended beneficiary, she does have rights. (B) is wrong because neither will help Physician in defense. The last statement deals with novation, the substitution of a new agreement (or party) for an old one. The reason this statement is an ineffectual defense is that it contains a false premise, which makes a novation impossible. The false premise is a contract between Betty and Physician ("Whatever contract Physician may have had with Betty . . ."). There is no contract between Betty and Physician! Betty's status as an intended beneficiary does confer some contractual rights, but it doesn't change the fact that there is no Betty-Physician agreement. If there is no Betty-Physician agreement, it can't be discharged by novation; there is nothing to discharge. The right answer is (D) because none of the statements is a good argument in defense.

26. More than 70 percent of my students select (D), which is wrong because it is an inaccurate statement of the law. Students see the promise to pay Dodge the $200 as gratuitous, meaning there is no consideration. However, there is valid consideration in the fact pattern. We are told that the money was in exchange for a promise not to sue. Each party benefits from the other's detriment. Dodge's detriment is foregoing a legal right (to sue) and his benefit is $200. Charles's detriment is paying $200, but as a result, he will not be a defendant in a lawsuit. (D) is partially correct in that Dodge will be unable to collect the remaining $50, but it is for the wrong reason. The reason Dodge can't collect is that he and Charles had a good faith dispute as to what was owed (we are told in the fact pattern that both parties "honestly believed," which implies good faith) and settled on $150. This settlement agreement is known as an "accord," which is "satisfied" by payment. Once Dodge accepted $150, the contract was discharged by performance and the correct answer is therefore (C).

27. This question is about something you probably discussed in the first few weeks of your Contracts course: theories of interpretation. The dominant theory and the one you need to know for the bar exam is that contracts are interpreted objectively; that is, how a reasonable person would understand the terms of the contract. This is a hard question because (A) is correct in noting the language is in fact a condition. The issue, however, is whether it can reasonably be expected that an insured would disclose a condition she didn't know she had, and clearly it is not. (B) is the correct answer because it offers the most reasonable interpretation of the condition, which the insured disclosed to the best of her knowledge.

28. The problem with (B) is that it misidentifies the condition that is precedent to performance. Joan's turning 21 doesn't trigger the insurance company's duty to pay; rather, it is the death of Mary that triggers performance. Students choosing (B) read the clause as Joan turning 21 as the triggering event. But if Joan turned 21 and her mother was still alive, the insurance company would not have to pay. It is Mary's death that is the condition that must occur before the insurance company pays. Joan's age has an impact on when performance occurs, not whether there is a duty to perform at all, and so (C) is the correct answer.

29. The mistake students make in choosing (A) is not having a complete understanding of the requirements for an anticipatory repudiation. Buyer's statement does not go far enough; while he said he was unhappy and did not intend to honor the contract, he also added language to the effect that he would honor the contract if required by law. That added language makes all the difference in this question because for an anticipatory repudiation, there has to be a clear, unequivocal assertion made by the party that he does not intend to perform. That is not the case here; Buyer said he would in fact perform if legally required, and the correct answer therefore is (D).

30. This is an extremely important question, and you can be sure an issue like this will appear on your exam. The bar examiners are testing a distinction between the UCC and common law, that of "perfect tender" and "substantial performance." Substantial performance is a common law concept. The UCC applies to this question because it involves the sale of goods. Whenever the bar examiners are testing a distinction, you can be sure that among the answer choices will be a correct answer for the wrong body of law. For example, in this case (A) would be correct under the common law. The mistake my students typically make involves a lack of complete understanding of the perfect tender rule, which is why (D) is also a wrong answer. The mistake is believing there is an automatic right to cure under the UCC. There is not. Under the perfect tender rule, the buyer has the right to reject if the goods fail in any respect to conform to the terms of the contract. The contract here was for delivery of 100 bushels of wheat on August 1. Ninety-five bushels were tendered, which therefore means the delivery was nonconforming, and so the correct answer is (C). There are two exceptions to the perfect tender rule, neither of which applies here. The seller has the right to cure if the time for performance has not yet expired. Here, delivery was tendered on the due date. If the 95 bushels were delivered on July 30, seller would have two days to cure and conform to the terms of the contract. The other exception applies when the seller delivers nonconforming goods but reasonably believes they will be acceptable to the buyer. In that case, if the tender is not acceptable, seller has a reasonable time to cure. Here, there is nothing in the fact pattern that suggests 95 bushels would be acceptable to the buyer.

31. This is another example of a UCC and common law distinction. (C) is the right answer under the common law of contracts, which requires consideration for option contracts. Without consideration, an offeror may revoke despite a promise to keep the offer open. However, this fact pattern involves a contract for the sale of goods and so the UCC applies. Option contracts do not require consideration under the UCC for options lasting no longer than three months. Here, the promise not to revoke was purportedly for one year. The mistake that students make is assuming the entire option is therefore void, which is incorrect. There is still an option for three months, and the offer is irrevocable for three months, which is why (B) is the correct answer.

32. The problem with (A) is that the June 2 telegram is an offer. There is a price term, quantity term, and delivery time and place. Under the objective theory of contract interpretation, a reasonable offeree could conclude that the telegram creates the power to accept. Even if one could make the case that the June 2 telegram was a price quote, this question reinforces the absolute necessity of reading carefully. We are looking for the *best* argument, which given the doubt of how to characterize the June 2 communication, (A) is therefore clearly not. The best way to approach a question like this is to define the status of the agreement after each communication. Given the discussion above about (A), let's begin with the premise that the June 1 communication was a solicitation for an offer and the June 2 telegram was an offer. Remember that the UCC is the source of law that governs here because we are dealing with the sale of goods. The acceptance on June 5 proposes a different term but is still valid. The question is whether the term becomes part of the contract, not whether or not there is a contract. Clearly, this would not be an acceptance under the common law because the acceptance isn't the mirror image of the offer. Under the UCC, however, we know that the offeror has the right to object to different terms, which was done by Vendor on June 6. So on June 6, we have a contract, the terms of which are contained in the June 2 correspondence. On June 9, the statement, "I don't deal with people . . ." may be read as a refusal to perform (repudiation and breach). Under the UCC, the repudiation by Bye Bye excuses Vendor's duty to perform, and the correct answer is (D).

Criminal Law

33. (D) illustrates two extremely important points about the bar exam. *(1) Never assume facts.* (D) is silent with respect to how crowded the streets were. Maybe it was 7:00 a.m. and there was nobody around. The facts are silent to where Abbott is located. Students selecting this answer did so because the Fourth of July triggered the image of crowded streets and that shooting into the streets filled with people is depraved heart. *(2) Make sure you understand the question.* Even if one could make a reasonable argument that this is in fact depraved heart/reckless indifference, it is still wrong because here you are asked where the defendant is *most likely* to be guilty of common law murder, meaning the best answer among the four given. (D) is arguably a close call, but there is no doubt that (B) is correct because the elements for felony murder have been satisfied. This question highlights the most common and avoidable error seen every year: **Intent to kill is not an element of common law murder.** Murder is the unlawful killing of a person with malice aforethought. That's the common law definition and there is no mention whatsoever about "intent." One way to prove malice aforethought is intent to kill, but there are three other ways, none of which require intent to kill: (1) intent to commit serious bodily injury; (2) depraved heart/ reckless indifference; and (3) felony murder. (B) is the correct answer because there was a killing during the commission of a dangerous felony, armed robbery. This is felony murder. The fact that defendant did

not intend to kill anyone is irrelevant because intent to kill is not an element of the crime.

34. Compare choice (A) in this question with choice (D) in the previous one. The distinctions are important. In the previous question, all we knew was that a pistol was discharged within city limits on the Fourth of July. Here, we are told that a rifle is fired into a house where the defendant knew a party was taking place. Firing a gun into the tight confines of a house where a party is taking place is not a close call. This is clearly depraved heart/reckless indifference and (A) is therefore the correct answer. The reason students incorrectly choose (B) is because they forget to consider voluntary manslaughter. The facts are ambiguous. We don't know if there was actual and reasonable provocation plus actual and reasonable lack of a cooling off period. That ambiguity alone is the reason why this isn't the choice most likely to be common law murder. It may very well be common law murder, but there is no doubt about choice (A).

35. Three initial points worth highlighting. First, you cannot answer this question correctly (at least without guessing) if you don't know the elements of robbery. You must know the elements of all the crimes tested on the bar exam. Second, knowing all the elements of the crimes tested on the MBE will get you zero points unless you practice applying that knowledge on questions like these. You are not being tested on your ability to memorize commercial outlines, and it bears repeating that one of the biggest mistakes you can make preparing for the bar exam is spending too much time reading outlines and watching videos at the expense of doing practice questions. Third — and this is the mistake students make in choosing (C) — you must read carefully! You are accustomed to looking for the *most* likely answer and it is easy to gloss over the fact that this question is looking for the *least* likely scenario. In other words, three of the answers are good because all the elements of robbery are present. Your task is to find the answer with one or more *missing elements*. Robbery is larceny plus two elements: (1) the property must be taken from the person or the person's presence and (2) the property must be taken by force or fear of force. (D) is the correct answer because the force element is missing. The slap at the end is a "red herring" because it has no connection with the crime. Students avoid choosing (D) because they see force but, again, the force has to be in relation to the robbery.

36. Students choosing (B) did not read the question carefully. Harry consented to the entry to *his own* house; he did not consent (nor did he have the power to consent) to the entry into *his neighbor's* house. This is a question about accomplice liability. For Harry to be convicted of burglary, he must have the requisite intent and perform some affirmative act in furtherance of that intent. Like many questions on the bar exam,

you should start with the basic elements. Burglary is the breaking and entering into the dwelling house of another at nighttime with the intent to commit a felony therein. The intent in this case involves stealing the silverware, but we are told in the fact pattern that the silverware belonged to Harry and he gave permission to Bill to take it. The permission negates the "intent to commit a felony therein" element, and the correct answer is therefore (D).

37. Which owner gave Bill consent, Harry or the neighbor? Clearly it was Harry and the consent was to break into his (Harry's) house. That consent does not get transferred to the neighbor's house. When we are looking for the best argument for acquittal, we are looking for something in the fact pattern that negates one of the elements of the crime. Here, if Bill thought he was in Harry's house, he did not have the intent to commit a felony because he was given permission to take Harry's silverware by someone who was authorized to give that permission: Harry. The correct answer is (C).

38. The mistake students make in choosing (A) is focusing on the "without permission" language. In the other three answer choices, the victim gave the defendant permission to use the property. Remember that the focus for property theft crime questions needs to be on the intent of the defendant. Larceny is the taking and carrying away the property of another with the intent to permanently deprive the owner of possession. In choice (A), Defendant did not have the intent to permanently deprive Owner of his property because we are told in the facts he intended to return the car. Without the intent to permanently deprive, Defendant may not be convicted of larceny. In (B), the correct answer, Defendant had the intent to permanently deprive Owner of his property at the time of the taking. That Defendant subsequently changed his mind doesn't undo or negate the crime.

39. If one didn't know the law, common sense would reasonably lead to the conclusion that (D) is correct under the playground rule of "no harm, no foul." Marty was going to give Joe the watch anyway. The purpose of this question is to test whether you recognize the irrelevancy of Marty's plan to give Joe the watch as a gift. As soon as Joe picked up the watch with the intent to permanently deprive Marty, the crime of larceny was completed. That is one mistake in reasoning students make in choosing (D). The other mistake is while recognizing there is a larceny issue, students reason the mere picking up of the watch does not satisfy the taking and carrying away element of the crime. Here's the rule you need to know for the bar exam and the reason why (A) is the correct answer: Any movement is enough. Picking up the watch satisfies the taking and carrying away element. It is irrelevant that Joe didn't put the watch in his pocket or take a step after picking up the watch.

40. The point about memorizing the levels of scrutiny and to which constitutional issues they attach similarly applies to many criminal law questions. You can pick up a lot of points simply by knowing the elements of crimes. *This is a big distinction between at-risk and other students.* Getting questions wrong is inevitable. You are not striving for a perfect score, you are striving for a passing score. That said, there really is no excuse for missing questions that are solely definitional. Good students will rarely get this question wrong because it requires very little reasoning and is in fact quite mechanical. There are three crimes listed in the answer choices. List the elements for each and see if they are present in the fact pattern. The crime at-risk students miss is burglary. I have seen two main mistakes made on this question in conjunction with burglary. The first is confusing larceny, robbery, and burglary. If one confuses robbery with burglary and knows that a defendant may not be convicted of robbery and larceny (because larceny is a lesser included offense), (B) would appear to be the correct answer. The other mistake students make is not having a complete understanding of the "breaking element" of burglary. Without a complete under- standing, it appears that Dirk didn't break into the apartment because John and Marsha took him in, according to the facts. The nuance you need to know for the bar exam is that the threat of force satisfies the breaking requirement, and so (A) is the correct answer.

41. The mistake students make in choosing (D) is related to a misunder- standing of causation. Dan intended to kill Tom and carried out that intent. Dan isn't exonerated because Tom had a pre-existing heart condition that also contributed to his death. Nor is it relevant that Tom would have died anyway in the plane crash had he been on board. Dan is guilty, as described in (A), because he killed Tom with intent. The heart condition and plane crash are there to distract you.

42. The subcategory of theft crimes is an example of an area where you may not see more than two or three questions, but it is well worth keeping these crimes straight because it is relatively easy. There is one more to add to the mix: larceny by trick. Larceny is all about unlawful possession (taking by trespass). It has nothing to do with obtaining title to goods. Larceny by trick is not a separate crime; rather, it is a method by which one may obtain unlawful possession (e.g., "May I borrow your car? I'll return it tomorrow," with no intention of ever returning). Contrast lar- ceny with false pretenses, where one obtains *title* to goods through a misrepresentation. Essentially, the only way the two crimes differ is by what is obtained: possession or ownership. Embezzlement is different from both because that crime is committed by one in lawful possession, like a trustee who is supposed to take care of someone else's money, but who then appropriates the goods for his own use. Finally, remember that robbery is larceny with two additional elements: person or person's presence plus force or threat thereof. This is extremely important because **the answer "defendant can be convicted of larceny *and* robbery" is always a wrong answer.** Larceny is a lesser included offense of robbery and one may not be convicted of both the greater and lesser included offense. The reason so many students choose (D) is that they didn't see any crime — because the money was paid. Paying fair market or even above fair market value doesn't negate the crime that already took place. (B) is the correct answer.

43. The mistake students make in choosing (D) is keying in on what the child died from — an illness. Their reasoning is that since the child died from an illness, the father could not have committed a crime. Here's a suggested "question" approach whenever you see a homicide question and are not provided a statute that defines the degrees of the crime (in other words, the common law applies): (1) Was the killing a murder? (2) If defendant intended to kill, can the murder be knocked down to voluntary manslaughter? (3) If the homicide wasn't a murder or voluntary manslaughter, apply the involuntary manslaughter analysis. In this case: Did the child die due to the father's gross negligence; that is, did the father disregard a substantial risk of death? The father knew the child was ill, had a duty to act because of the "special relationship" (father and son), and failed to do so, disregarding a substantial risk. Therefore, the correct answer is (B).

44. Every fact is potentially critical on the bar exam. Tellers do not normally laugh at bank robbers. Did you ask yourself why you were told the teller laughed and how it had any bearing on the question? Most of my students do not. The criminal charge here is robbery. What is the connection between laughter and robbery? One of the elements of robbery is the use of force or threat of force or putting the victim in fear. A laughing teller is not a fearful teller. For Paul to be convicted of the underlying crime (robbery) as Jack's accomplice, all the elements of common law robbery must be established. If they are not, Paul is a free man. (D) is the right answer because it recognizes that one of the elements of the crime has been negated.

Evidence

45. Approximately two-thirds of my students miss this question every year, almost all of whom believe (D) is the correct answer. Parker certainly made a statement and it certainly was made under belief of impending death. Let's go through the hearsay analysis. The out of court statement, "make sure my estate collects the $10,000 I loaned to Davidson," is being offered for the truth of the matter asserted therein, that Davidson owed Parker $10,000. The statement is therefore hearsay. However, the

statement is *inadmissible hearsay* because the dying declaration exception doesn't apply to this statement. The detailed requirements for application of hearsay exceptions are critical to know for bar exam success. Hearsay makes up one-third of all the MBE evidence questions. Dying declarations are admissible in homicide prosecutions or in civil cases *when they concern the cause or circumstance of death*. Here, the dying declaration is about collection of a debt, which has nothing to do with the manner of death, and so the correct answer is (B).

46. (C) is absolutely a true statement of fact: The consultant is not an attorney. Here's the rule you need to know for the bar exam, though, and the reason (A) is the right answer: communications between a lawyer's client and an investigator who is the lawyer's agent are generally protected by the attorney-client privilege.

47. A present sense impression must be immediate. Ten minutes is too long to be considered a present sensory observation, which is why (B) is a wrong answer. Is five minutes too long? Yes. How about one minute or 30 seconds? I don't know and neither do the bar examiners. The point is that if the bar examiners are testing present sense impression, the time lapse will not be a close call. While the present sense impression exception is inapplicable, (B) is correct in identifying the statement as hearsay. The problem is that it is inadmissible hearsay. Here we have a statement to the effect that "Dorry caused the accident" offered to prove the truth of the matter asserted, that Dorry was the one who hit the plaintiff. Since none of the exceptions apply, (C) is the correct answer.

48. The mistake students made in choosing (A) is an erroneous understanding of the doctor-patient privilege. The privilege *exclusively* belongs to the patient. This is similar to the attorney-client privilege. The privilege does not belong to the lawyer; rather, it belongs *exclusively* to the client. This is an example of a very difficult question that requires careful reading and the process of elimination to get to the right answer because none of the choices presented are particularly good. This illustrates the situation where you have to select "the least wrong answer." Take another look at the question. You are not being asked for the *right* answer. You are being asked for the best answer of the four given to you. There is a significant distinction between "right" and "best" with which you must become comfortable. Otherwise, you will lose valuable time trying to figure out the right answer where it doesn't exist. (B) has to be wrong because the patient is not the person exercising the privilege and we know that the privilege belongs exclusively to the patient. (C) should strike you as making no sense because whether or not a patient receives some form of affirmative treatment is absolutely irrelevant to the application of the doctor-patient privilege. This is analogous to a client leaving a lawyer's office without receiving legal advice. The communication is still privileged. That leaves (D), the least wrong answer because we

may reasonably assume the attorney is acting on behalf or in the best interests of his client. Again, (D) is not right; rather, it is the best answer and that is what we are told to look for.

49. More than three-fourths of students get this question wrong. First, do you see why (B) is clearly a wrong answer? (B) is a misstatement or an incomplete statement of the law. Dying declarations may also be used in civil cases. The majority of students choose (C), which is a tempting answer, but contains a fundamental mistake about the then-existing state of mind exception to the hearsay rule you may pick up with careful reading. The exception for the then-existing mental condition refers to the declarant's statement, in this case Pedestrian's. The affidavit is the doctor's statement. Pedestrian's statement is hearsay and the affidavit is also hearsay. Yet the affidavit may be considered by the court and so the correct answer is (D). This question isn't about whether Pedestrian's statement itself is admissible, but whether the judge may consider hearsay in determining the admissibility of evidence, and the answer is yes.

50. The first step in any hearsay question is to identify the out of court statement and then determine the purpose for which it is being offered. If it is offered for its truth value, it is hearsay. If the statement is offered for a reason other than its truth value, it's not hearsay. (Remember that a statement that is not hearsay may still be inadmissible for some other reason.) This question is simply testing whether you are aware of the hearsay exception stated in the correct answer, (A). The out of court statement (the records) are being offered for their truth value: that defendant was not in fact incarcerated on the date in question. The statement is inadmissible unless an exception or exclusion applies, and the Federal Rules of Evidence provide an exception for the absence of an entry from the public record. The mistake students make in choosing (D) is simply not knowing the exception. If such an exception did not exist, (D) probably would be correct and all of the records searched would need to be produced.

51. Every hearsay question should receive the same basic analysis. Here, we have an out of court statement made by Defendant to her friend to the effect that she, the defendant, would be out of town. The statement is being offered to prove the truth of the matter asserted therein, that Defendant was indeed out of town at the time of the robbery. The statement is therefore hearsay and the majority of students end their analysis here, incorrectly selecting (D). However, the next step in the analysis is to determine whether the hearsay comes in as an exception or exemption to the general rule. Here, the statement comes in under the then-existing state of mind exception. A statement that is otherwise hearsay may be admissible to show the intent or plan of the defendant. Here, the statement comes in as evidence of intent to be out of town at the time of the robbery, and the correct answer is therefore (B).

52. The first step in any hearsay question is to run through this analysis: *(1) Is there a statement?* Here, the statement is, "[defendant is] my partner in this." *(2) Is the statement offered for the truth of the matter asserted therein or is it being offered for some other reason?* Here, the statement is being offered to prove the truth of the matter asserted, that defendant was in fact Seller's partner. *(3) If the statement was offered for its truth value, does the statement meet the requirements for an exception and therefore admissible despite being hearsay?* Here, there's no applicable exception, and the error students make is stopping their analysis here and choosing (B). Remember, there is another step: *(4) If the statement was offered for its truth value, is that statement excluded by definition from the hearsay rule and therefore* not hearsay? Here's a very good example of the need to read and think actively and critically. Why is it important that we are told in the fact pattern that the defendant was silent? Silence in the hearsay context should raise the issue of adoptive admission, which is not hearsay by rule. Ask yourself whether a reasonable person would object if the statement was false. We would expect someone who wasn't a partner in this crime to say so when introduced that way. The correct answer is (D).

53. The takeaway lesson of this question is that the bar exam tests details, not general concepts. (B) is wrong for *two* distinct reasons. (1) The past recollection recorded exception requires, among other things, that the declarant is testifying as a witness. Here, we are told that the declarant died before trial so the exception cannot apply. (2) The exception also requires a memorandum or recording; in other words, something that can be read or played. Here, we have neither because a sketch is not capable of being read or played into evidence. Therefore, the correct answer is (C). The teller's out of court statement, the sketch, is being offered to prove the truth of the matter asserted therein, that the person sketched is Miller. Note that the prior identification exclusion does not apply. Do you see why? That exclusion only applies to a witness who is testifying. Our witness is dead.

54. The two statements are certainly consistent and one occurred prior to the other, which is why the vast majority of students select (B). Again, you need to know the requirements for the exceptions and exemptions, a matter of pure memorization, which can result in easy points on the bar exam. The statement that Miller had never been in the bank is clearly hearsay because it is being offered to prove the truth of the matter asserted therein, that he had never been in the bank that was robbed. Prior consistent statements are exempt from the hearsay rule, but all the requirements for exclusion must be met. This is purely definitional and easy (but not intuitive). By rule, a prior consistent statement cannot come in unless the credibility of the witness is attacked. Miller is testifying on direct examination; there has been no attack on his credibility. The testimony is therefore inadmissible hearsay, and the correct answer is (C).

Real Property

55. For those of you who feel intimidated by future interests, this is an excellent example of why knowing a few definitions can be extremely beneficial. First of all, whenever you see a conveyance, you should always stop to define the present and future interests. Here, Selden has a life estate ("to my son Selden for life"). The future interest is a remainder in Selden's children. The first issue is the kind of remainder the children have — contingent or vested. We are told that Selden already has two adult children, so those children have a vested remainder. They are certain to take an interest in the farm when Selden dies. What you should see is that the remainder is to a class ("children") not just to the two children already in existence. During his life plus nine months, Selden can have more children. If he does in fact have more children, what happens to the remainder the two ascertained children have? Nothing, because the remainder is vested. But the *amount* of their financial interest in the farm will be reduced with each successive child fathered by Selden. So the remainder is vested, but the amount each child will take is uncertain. (A) is incorrect for that very reason. The question is not whether the two current adult children take under the will; the question is how much they will take because the value of their shares will decrease with each of Selden's additional children. Since their share amount is not fixed, (C) is the correct answer.

56. This is a very useful learning question in which three times as many students pick the same wrong answer than students who answer correctly. The takeaway point is that exact language is particularly important when it comes to property conveyances. This looks like a defeasible fee. Remember that there are three defeasible fees: the fee simple determinable, the fee simple subject to a condition subsequent, and the fee simple subject to an executory interest. To defease the fee, specific language is required in the conveyance. Look for "so long as" (determinable); "but if" and "subject to the right of re-entry" (subject to a condition subsequent); and "but if" and "then to" (subject to an executory limitation). The problem with (B) and the reason why (C) is the right answer is that the magic words are missing: "Subject to the understanding" is not the same thing as "but if" and "subject to the right of re-entry." I think of future interests as the big bully everyone in class is afraid of, but really it is not so tough. Future interests are intimidating because the language is difficult, but many students miss easy points because as soon as they see a future interest issue, they think RAP and panic. Most future interest questions will not have anything to do with

the RAP, so before you give up on a question, remember that much of future interests is very mechanical. Identify the present estate and the magic words needed to create the corresponding future interest.

57. Three times as many of my students selected (A) than selected the correct answer, (D). The issue in this fact pattern is the responsibility of life tenants in possession. Property is all about rules. What makes (A) so tempting is that you know that, as a general rule, life tenants have certain responsibilities, like not committing waste, paying the interest on the mortgage, and the like, and it seems reasonable to assume there is a similar responsibility to pay real estate taxes. Life tenants are in fact responsible for paying real estate taxes, but do you see something about the property here that probably differs from most real property questions you have seen held in a life estate? This property is totally vacant and unused. Lena isn't deriving *any* benefit from the property by living there or through rental income. The rule that you need to know is that *life tenants are responsible for taxes for the fair market rental value of the property if occupied by the life tenant or for taxes based on the actual rental income received by the life tenant.* Here, the holder of the life estate does not have any real estate tax burden because she doesn't occupy or otherwise derive financial benefit through rental of the property.

58. (A) is tempting because it contains a true statement. Let's say Olive conveyed the life estate to Lois in 1995, fifteen years ago. Lois lived in Blackacre for a year and then leased the property to Trent in 1996 for a term of fifteen years ending in 2011. Lois's life estate terminated in 1999, when she died. What was the future interest that became possessory when Lois died? Olive had a reversion. The mistake in (A) is that while it is true that Olive held a reversion when Lois died, Olive subsequently lost title. This is the key piece students miss. Upon Lois's death, Olive holds title in fee simple. But Olive does not take possession of the land, even though she has the right to. Ron, Lois's heir, begins to adversely possess the land in 1999 when Lois died and Trent began paying rent to Ron. Ron is holding himself out as the owner of Blackacre by accepting rent payment from Trent, who continues to be a tenant. In 2009, Ron acquires title to Blackacre by adverse possession (adverse to Olive who never exercised her right of possession), and the correct answer is therefore (C).

59. Recall the difference between distributions per stirpes and distributions per capita. Per capita distributions treat each survivor equally, while per stirpes distributions treat each family branch equally. Assume I leave my estate to my heirs and I have two children, A and B, and B has three children, X, Y, and Z. My child B predeceases me. Under a per stirpes distribution, A would take 50 percent of my estate and X, Y, and Z would split B's 50 percent share equally, each taking one-third of one-half (or one-sixth) of the total distribution. Under a per capita distribution, A, X,

Y, and Z would each take a 25 percent share of the distribution. We are told in the fact pattern that Della has a life estate and the future interest is a remainder. There are two types of remainders: contingent remainders and vested remainders. If a remainder is contingent, some stated condition must be met before the remaindermen can take possession or one or more of the remaindermen is unascertained. A vested remainder is one given to an ascertained person and not subject to a prior condition; it becomes possessory upon the death of the life estate holder. Here, we are told the remainder is contingent and have to identify the rationale for the court's conclusion. The mistake my students made in choosing (B) was not understanding the distinction between remainders. If the remainder vested upon Theresa's death, the remainder would be just that: vested. We know with certainty who Theresa's descendants are when she dies and the remainder could not be contingent upon anything. The reason why (C) is correct is related to the definition of contingent remainders, that some condition must be met before the remainder becomes possessory. If there were no condition, the remainder would be vested, which is contrary to the facts. Here, the only answer that identifies a condition is (C). If the remainder is contingent, it has to be contingent upon survivors.

60. The best way to go about answering this question is defining the property interest each time there is a conveyance. In this question, we are concerned about the real property. In 1950, Orris holds title to Brownacre in fee simple and Hull begins to adversely possess. We are told the period to obtain title by adverse possession is ten years, so in 1960, Hull has title in fee. Hull still has title in 1962 because we are told the transfer of the real property to Burns was ineffective. 1n 1963, Burns leases Brownacre from Orris for five years. Oriss's adverse possession begins. Hull still has title. In 1967, the Orris to Burns lease ends. Hull still has title. Burns begins to adversely possess Brownacre. In 1970, Burns leaves. Hull still has title. In 1970, Orris quitclaims Brownacre to Powell. (D) is wrong because Orris didn't have a property interest in Brownacre to convey. In 1960, Hull obtained title by adverse possession and never lost title; therefore, (A) is correct. Orris began to adversely possess the land in 1963, but didn't hold Brownacre adversely for ten years, the required statutory period.

Torts

61. This question is about causation, and you should always start with the applicable test. For actual causation with only one cause, we apply the "but for" test. If we can say "but for the defendant's negligence, the harm would not have occurred," actual causation is present. Here, we can say that but for the driver negligently swerving his car, the

fire hydrant would not have been damaged. Students who incorrectly chose (B) were correct on the actual causation issue. The second step in the analysis, though, is to determine whether there is proximate causation, which turns on the question of foreseeability. Here's where students go wrong in their analysis. Students incorrectly apply the foreseeability test and conclude that it is not foreseeable that a fire hydrant would be damaged by a swerving car. That conclusion is inappropriately narrow in focus. The issue is not whether a fire hydrant would be specifically damaged, but whether property damage is a foreseeable result of negligently swerving a car. Clearly it is, and the correct answer is therefore (A).

The best way I have found to solidify the concept of proximate cause for students having difficulty is by using the "flaming rat" example. Perhaps you read this case in law school: A young man was cleaning a vending machine with a gasoline-soaked rag in a small room with a heater. A rat in the vending machine ran out, got too close to the heater, and caught fire. The rat ran back into the vending machine, causing an explosion which killed the young man (and presumably the rat). Can you imagine a more unforeseeable set of circumstances? Herein lies the rule you need to know: Foreseeability is about the harm that resulted, not the manner in which the harm occurred. A flaming rat running into a vending machine is completely unforeseeable. But what about the harm that resulted — an exploding vending machine? The question is not whether the rat is foreseeable; the question is whether it is foreseeable that a vending machine may explode while being cleaned with a gasoline-soaked rag in a small enclosed space containing an open heater. Proximate cause is all about the "f-word" — foreseeability. Highly improbable scenarios often lead students astray because the manner of harm is clearly unforeseeable. Proximate cause foreseeability is not focused on the manner of harm, but on the foreseeability of the resulting harm itself. The "flaming rat" is particularly useful to remember.

62. Assumption of risk is a tempting answer, but remember, the bar exam is notorious for testing exceptions and limitations to general rules. This is the rule you need to know for the bar exam: The assumption of risk doctrine does not apply to rescuers so (C) must be a wrong answer. The reason (B) is correct is that rescuers are always foreseeable.

63. This question further reinforces why it is so important to read carefully. We are told that we are in a pure comparative fault jurisdiction. You must ask yourself why this matters, why this piece of information is important. To begin with, recall that in pure comparative fault the plaintiff may recover damages no matter what her degree of fault. For example, if plaintiff is 90 percent at fault, defendant is 10 percent at fault, and total damages are $1,000, the plaintiff will recover $100. It doesn't matter that plaintiff was more at fault than defendant. The

question asks whether Mechanic will obtain a judgment against Basher, which is different from the question of which party is most at fault. In a pure comparative jurisdiction, it doesn't matter. The reason (B) is wrong is that even if Adam was negligent in failing to warn, that doesn't mean that Basher isn't also negligent (or, for that matter, the mechanic if using the hammer to loosen the material). If Basher was negligent with respect to Mechanic, Mechanic will obtain a judgment against Basher even if Basher was only 1 percent at fault. Note also that the correct answer (D) doesn't definitively state that Basher was negligent with respect to Mechanic, only that Mechanic would receive a judgment if Basher was negligent.

64. In order for Motorist to be liable, he must have been negligent. The lesson here is that before assigning liability, make sure you can articulate the breach of duty. Motorists have a duty to use reasonable care when driving, but what specifically did Motorist do that was a breach of that duty? Is having a heart attack a breach of the duty to use reasonable care? It could be, if Motorist was on notice that he was at risk of having a heart attack, but there is nothing in the fact pattern to so indicate. In fact, we are specifically told Motorist had no history of heart disease and no warning of the attack (like prior chest pains, for example). Motorist did not breach his duty to use reasonable care (i.e., he was not negligent) and therefore is not liable. The mistake students make in choosing (D) is the failure to recognize that accidents sometimes happen without negligence. Without evidence of negligence, the case will not make it to the jury, and the correct answer is therefore (C).

65. Do you see the essence of this question? Whether a cause is intervening or superseding is about foreseeability. If subsequent negligent conduct is foreseeable, it is deemed an intervening cause. If, however, the subsequent act was unforeseeable, it is deemed a superseding cause. Why does it matter? An intervening cause does not relieve the first negligent actor of liability, while a superseding cause relieves the first negligent actor of any liability. Here, there are two causes of Price's injuries: the defective bolt and Dunn's negligent driving. The issue is whether Dunn's negligence was foreseeable and turns on the foreseeability of car accidents. Car accidents are a foreseeable consequence of driving. In fact, they are highly foreseeable, and regulations like seatbelt laws are enacted to protect motor vehicle occupants when accidents occur. The foreseeability of car accidents prompts these and similar safety regulations. The car accident, as a result of Dunn's negligence, was foreseeable and doesn't absolve Motorco from liability due to the defective bolt, and so the correct answer is (A). Without even reading the fact pattern, you should recognize that (B) must be a wrong answer. Do you see why? (B) and (C) are the same answer! Proximate cause is legal cause. There can only be *one* right answer on the bar exam, so when you see two answers that are the same, they both have to be wrong. There is yet another reason (B) is wrong: (B) implies there may only be one proximate cause of harm, which we know to be untrue. There may be multiple intervening causes of harm.

66. Like offer and acceptance, negligence, particularly the nuances of causation, are a must-win on the bar exam. Negligence is the most tested category on the MBE, and you must maximize points in this category because the concepts are not that difficult and you can't afford to miss these points, like my students did on this question. (C) would probably be the obvious answer for someone who didn't go to law school because it looks like the common sense approach. Dever had absolutely nothing to do with *causing* the fire to start. However, the issue isn't whether Dever caused the fire. The issue is whether Dever has *any* responsibility for the damage caused by the fire and the answer is yes. My students failed to characterize the car accident as an intervening act of negligence, the result of which worsened the damage caused by the fire. Dever's failure to exercise reasonable care caused damage in excess of what otherwise would have occurred but for his negligence. The correct answer is therefore (A). You should also recognize that while Dever's act was an intervening cause, it was not a superseding cause that would break the causational chain between the first negligent actor (the fire starter) and the damage. Car accidents are a foreseeable consequence when emergency vehicles are rushing to a fire.

67. This is another question about foreseeability. My students were thrown off because they see construction sites all the time where equipment is left scattered around. A common practice may nevertheless be negligent. So let's assume it is unreasonable care to leave a ladder against the side of a house while the occupants are away. The next question is whether or not it is foreseeable that a thief could then use the ladder to break into the house. In fact, this is exactly the type of harm one could imagine by leaving a ladder on the side of an unoccupied house and the roofer will be liable under general negligence principles, and so (B) is correct.

68. Notice the twist on the typical negligence per se question. Usually, it is the defendant who has violated a statute and the plaintiff introduces the violation as evidence of negligence. Here, the defendant is using the *plaintiff's* violation to defeat plaintiff's cause of action. But what was the cause of the harm here, the earlier arrival point or Driver's negligent operation of his vehicle? While it is factually true, as (C) suggests, that Walker was in the crosswalk, that isn't the reason her earlier violation will not defeat her cause of action. Walker was in the crosswalk and the light was in her favor; in other words, the violation of the statute was not the cause of her injuries. By way of analogy, assume a driver was

speeding before slowing down and proceeding within posted limits. Driver proceeds through a green light in his favor when struck by another driver who went through a red light. The first driver would have not been in the intersection had he been driving within the speed limit earlier. Does that mean that the first driver's cause of action will be defeated for violating the speed limit? No, the cause of the accident was the second driver's negligence, not the speed limit violation. The correct answer is therefore (D).

69. The key point to take away from this question is that a bad outcome does not automatically mean a doctor was negligent. The problem with (B) is that there is nothing to suggest the doctor did anything wrong. Without evidence of negligence, the formation of a blood clot, while unfortunate, does not result in automatic liability. The operation itself wasn't "negligent," as (B) suggests. What was the alleged act of negligence in these facts? It was the failure to consult with a cardiologist. But even if that failure was negligent on the part of the doctor, plaintiff still doesn't win without proving a causal connection between the failure to consult and her harm. (C) is the only answer choice that correctly reflects that the burden on the plaintiff is to show that consultation would have prevented the clot.

70. The burdens of production and persuasion, which are collectively referred to as the "burden of proof," are extremely important concepts to understand. When the bar examiners ask whether a court will grant a motion for a directed verdict (a very commonly asked question on the MBE), they are testing these concepts, often in the context of the doctrine *res ipsa loquitur*. When we say that the plaintiff has the burden of proof in civil cases, there are really two burdens she must meet, one of which may shift to the defendant, the other of which *never* shifts to the defendant. The plaintiff presents her evidence at the beginning of a civil trial and has the burden of production, also known as the "burden of establishing a prima facie case." In a negligence claim, the plaintiff must meet her burden of production with respect to each element of negligence: duty, breach, causation, and damages. The nature of the burden is that plaintiff must present enough evidence that a reasonable juror, drawing all reasonable inferences in favor of the plaintiff, could decide for plaintiff on all four elements.

The question of whether or not the plaintiff has met the burden of production is a *legal* question. The judge, not the jury, decides. At the close of plaintiff's negligence case, defendant will almost always move for a directed verdict, asking the judge to dismiss plaintiff's case because as a matter of law she did not introduce sufficient evidence to meet her burden of production.

If the motion for a directed verdict is denied, and the defendant doesn't present any evidence, one of two things may happen. First, the case may go to the jury. Even though the plaintiff has met her burden of production, she still bears the burden of persuasion. She has the burden of proving all four elements of the negligence claim by a preponderance of the evidence. Second, the judge may grant a directed verdict in favor of the *plaintiff* because her evidence is so overwhelming with respect to each element of the claim that no reasonable juror could find for the defendant as a matter of law. The following representation may be helpful:

A (0)	B (25)	C (50)	D (75)	E (100)

Plaintiff starts the trial at point A with the burden of production. She must establish a prima facie case by introducing sufficient evidence such that a reasonable juror, drawing all reasonable inferences in favor of the plaintiff, could decide for her on all of four elements of the negligence claim. Graphically, she must cross point B on all four elements. If she fails to cross point B on one or more element, she will lose on defendant's motion for a directed verdict as a matter of law and never gets her case before the jury. If plaintiff satisfies the elements of negligence per se, she has met her burden of production with respect to duty and breach. She must still produce evidence of causation and damages or will lose as a matter of law. If plaintiff meets her burden with respect to each element, she does not automatically win. All it means is that she has met her production burden and will survive a directed verdict motion.

In the fact pattern above, the representative did not offer *any* evidence as to what the defendant did wrong (the breach of duty), which makes (A) a tempting choice. This is where the doctrine of *res ipsa loquitur* comes in. *Res ipsa loquitur,* "the thing speaks for itself," allows the plaintiff to survive a motion to dismiss despite not offering any specific evidence pointing to a breach of duty, if the following three conditions are met: The accident or harm does not ordinarily occur absent negligence; the defendant was in sole control of the instrumentality that caused the harm; and the plaintiff was not contributorily negligent. In our fact pattern, there is no evidence of wrongdoing; only that the plane crashed. Applying *res ipsa,* planes do not ordinarily crash absent negligence, the plane was in the sole control of the airline, and plaintiff was not contributorily negligent. The correct answer is (C) because *res ipsa* has allowed the plaintiff to meet her burden of production; now it is up to the jury to determine whether each element has been proven by a preponderance of evidence.

Assuming the plaintiff has met the burden of production, the defendant may decide not to present a case but to argue that plaintiff has not met her burden of persuasion (a preponderance of the evidence) for each element. The jury decides the case and must determine whether plaintiff has produced sufficient evidence to cross point C for each element. If the jury finds for the plaintiff, plaintiff has met her burdens of production AND persuasion. If the jury finds for defendant, plaintiff has met her burden of production, but not her burden of persuasion. If the plaintiff produces a case that goes well beyond the burden of production so as to be overwhelming by crossing point D, the burden of *production* will shift to defendant, which means that if defendant doesn't present rebuttal evidence, defendant will lose as a matter of law. The defendant must get the case back to the left of point D. The burden of persuading the jury (when the case ends up between points B and D), never shifts from the plaintiff to the defendant. The plaintiff must prove each element of her case crosses point C.

71. More than half of my students found for the passenger's representative, and the majority of the students believed that the failure to provide the statutorily required preservers made the ocean liner negligent per se. Do you see the faulty reasoning? The ocean liner *was* negligent per se but was *not* liable. The purpose of the statute was to protect passengers from drowning, exactly the harm that occurred here, and the plaintiff is clearly a member of the class the statute was designed to protect, cruise ship passengers. However, negligent conduct does not necessarily result in liability for negligence. Negligence per se applies to the first two elements of a negligence claim by establishing a breach of duty. Plaintiffs must still introduce evidence of causation and damages. Negligent conduct is a breach of duty. Liability for negligence requires that the breach of duty caused plaintiff's damages. This is a question about causation and the issue is whether the negligent conduct of the cruise liner caused the death of the passenger. Application of the test for actual causation leads to the conclusion that the cruise liner's negligence *was not* the cause of death: Can one say that "but for the absence of the statutorily required lifeboats, the passenger would not have drowned"? No, because the facts tell us that the passenger would have drowned even if the lifeboats were present. If the passenger would have drowned anyway, the absence of the lifeboats could not have actually caused the passenger's death and the correct answer is therefore (C).

72. The claim for negligent infliction of emotional distress causes much confusion, centered mainly on the concepts of physical impact and physical manifestation of injury. The majority rule is based on the so-called Zone of Danger (ZOD). If a plaintiff is in the ZOD and not directly injured by defendant's negligent conduct, it is nevertheless foreseeable she may have been injured and she may recover for a "near miss" *if* she can prove physical manifestations of distress (an upset stomach is enough). If plaintiff is outside of the ZOD, in an area where her risk of injury was unforeseeable, she may only recover if she is in close proximity

and witnesses an accident involving a close family member. There are two exceptions where a plaintiff may recover notwithstanding these rules: (1) a plaintiff may recover damages for emotional distress for the negligent handling of the corpse of a close family member despite not witnessing it and (2) a plaintiff may recover damages when mistakenly informed of the death of a close family member.

By way of example, assume a minor was injured when struck by an automobile whose driver was negligent. The minor was rendered bloody and unconscious. There were several people in the general area of the accident: Pedestrian 1, a stranger, was standing next to the minor when he was hit. Pedestrian 2, also a stranger, was located a couple of blocks away from the minor and witnessed the accident. Mother was a block away and witnessed the accident. Father was home, also a block away but in the other direction, and was immediately notified about the accident and rushed to his injured and bloody child.

P1 may recover for the "near miss" if he can prove physical manifestations of distress. He was in the ZOD; it was foreseeable that he may have suffered injury as a result of the driver's negligence. P2 may not recover despite physical manifestations of distress; he was neither in the ZOD nor was he a close relative of the minor. Mother may recover even though she was outside of the ZOD because she was close to the accident site and witnessed the accident involving a close family relative. Father will not recover, despite being near the site of the accident and the minor was his child because he did not actually see the accident when it occurred.

In the question here, students tend to jump at choice (D) because of the physical harm suffered as a result of the emotional distress. The problem with this answer choice is that the restaurateur was not in the ZOD, and therefore was neither physically injured nor suffered physical manifestations of emotional distress from a near miss. The rule that you need to know for the bar exam is that property damage alone will not support a claim for emotional distress, and the correct answer is therefore (C).

73. Why do you think you were specifically told in the fact pattern that the rifle and bullets were stolen from a *locked* cabinet? Every word is potentially critical to answering a bar exam question correctly. The mistake my students made was focusing on Del's failure to activate the motion detector. For Paula to prevail, she must prove that Del had a duty to use reasonable care, failed to use reasonable care, and that failure caused her injuries. If the cabinet was left open or unlocked, Del clearly would have been negligent. But here Del took reasonable care by locking the cabinet. That he could have also set the alarm doesn't make him liable by negating the reasonable care he took in locking the cabinet,

which is why (A) is wrong. (D) is the correct answer because had Del been on notice that his store was in a high crime area, had frequently been broken into, had guns stolen despite the cabinet being locked, and the like, then he would have breached his duty to exercise reasonable care by failing to set the alarm.

Chapter 6

Conclusion

Some final thoughts and tips as you move toward the beginning of your commercial bar review course.

1. **You should realistically assess your strengths and weaknesses.** Maximize your strengths and identify areas where you are weak that really matter. But remember, there are certain areas you simply cannot concede despite being weak. These areas are: negligence; individual rights; constitutional protections afforded the accused; hearsay; presentation of evidence; formation of contracts; and performance, breach, and discharge of contracts. These seven areas combined account for about 80 questions, or 40 percent, of the MBE.

2. **The best answer is not always perfect.** Remember that you are looking for the best answer among the four choices you are provided. The "right" answer may not always be among the choices, but there will always be one answer that is better than the other three.

3. **You must read carefully.** I hope you have been persuaded by the many examples of how careless reading costs valuable points. Most people who fail the bar exam come within a handful of points of passing. You do not want to fail because you were careless.

4. **Don't over-rely on substantive outlines at the expense of doing practice questions.** You need to learn the law in the context of fact patterns because that is what you will be tested on. Go through questions and answer choices systematically and methodically. Understand why every wrong answer is wrong, even if you answered the question correctly, before you move on to the next question. As a result, you will not only increase your substantive knowledge of the law but also how it is applied, or misapplied, on actual questions.

5. **The bar exam is "pass/fail."** You must be strategic in your studies and during the exam itself. The goal is not to answer all the questions correctly, but to maximize your score. Do not let yourself get stuck on a hard question. You will waste valuable time and lose confidence. Take your best shot by eliminating any obviously wrong answers and move on. If you don't know the answer in two minutes, the odds are

you will not know the answer in three, four, or five minutes. When you get stuck, you are taking time away from other questions. Hard questions are not worth more than easy questions. Every question is worth the same one point.

6. **Answering bar exam questions is a skill and, like most skills, you will only get better with practice.**

I hope this book provided a solid start to your bar preparation efforts.